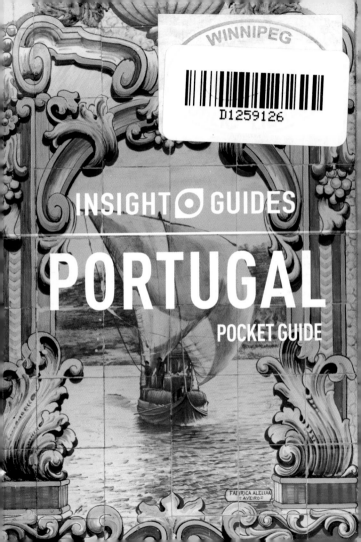

D1259126

INSIGHT ⊙ GUIDES

PORTUGAL

POCKET GUIDE

FABRICA ALELUIA
AVEIRO

Walking Eye App

YOUR FREE EBOOK AVAILABLE THROUGH THE WALKING EYE APP

Your guide now includes a free eBook to your chosen destination, for the same great price as before. Simply download the Walking Eye App from the App Store or Google Play to access your free eBook.

HOW THE WALKING EYE APP WORKS

Through the Walking Eye App, you can purchase a range of eBooks and destination content. However, when you buy this book, you can download the corresponding eBook for free. Just see below in the grey panel where to find your free content and then scan the QR code at the bottom of this page.

Destinations: Download essential destination content featuring recommended sights and attractions, restaurants, hotels and an A–Z of practical information, all available for purchase.

Ships: Interested in ship reviews? Find independent reviews of river and ocean ships in this section, all available for purchase.

eBooks: You can download your free accompanying digital version of this guide here. You will also find a whole range of other eBooks, all available for purchase.

Free access to travel-related blog articles about different destinations, updated on a daily basis.

HOW THE EBOOKS WORK

The eBooks are provided in EPUB file format. Please note that you will need an eBook reader installed on your device to open the file. Many devices come with this as standard, but you may still need to install one manually from Google Play.

The eBook content is identical to the content in the printed guide.

HOW TO DOWNLOAD THE WALKING EYE APP

1. Download the Walking Eye App from the App Store or Google Play.
2. Open the app and select the scanning function from the main menu.
3. Scan the QR code on this page – you will then be asked a security question to verify ownership of the book.
4. Once this has been verified, you will see your eBook in the purchased ebook section, where you will be able to download it.

Other destination apps and eBooks are available for purchase separately or are free with the purchase of the Insight Guide book.

TOP 10 ATTRACTIONS

COIMBRA
The historic university city has been the hub of Portugal's intellectual life since the 13th century. See page 55.

SINTRA
Magical mansions, fantastical palaces, and gardens of delight in Lisbon's aristocratic summer retreat. See page 40.

BELÉM
Pay homage to Portuguese explorers and eat custard tarts in Lisbon's riverside district. See page 37.

TRÁS-OS-MONTES
Witness Portuguese tradition in these remote and beautiful farmlands. See page 88.

BOM JESUS DO MONTE
A place of pilgrimage with a stairway to heaven in the mountains of the Minho. See page 83.

PORTO
Portugal's historic second city, straddling the River Douro, is keeping pace with the 21st century. See page 64.

ALGARVE
The Mediterranean climate and golden beaches have made it Portugal's top destination for sunseekers. See page 107.

DOURO VALLEY
One of Portugal's prettiest regions and home to the renowned port wine. See page 73.

SERRA DA ESTRELA
Hikes amid fantastic scenery in Portugal's highest mountains. See page 62.

ÉVORA
Once a Roman settlement, now a star of the Alentejo. See page 97.

A PERFECT TOUR

Day 1

The north

Start in northern
Portugal, exploring the
magnificent baroque
and tile-coated
buildings of Porto, and
sampling the finest port
wines. Alternatively
start your journey in the
lovely university town
of Coimbra, a chance to
see its wonderful jumble
of historic architecture,
and hear the city's
unique melancholy *fado*.

Day 3

Heading south

Take a leisurely drive down to Lisbon, calling in at
fascinating Tomar on the way – its Templar castle is
a Unesco World Heritage Site and well worth a look.
Once at the capital, book into the Bairro Alto Hotel (see
page 180) for an upmarket treat.

Day 4

In the capital

Indulge in some retail
therapy at the Colombo
Centre in the morning,
then while away the
afternoon in Belém,
seeing the fantastical
Mosteiro dos Jerónimos
and eating Portugal's
most perfect custard
tarts. In the evening,
either head to a *fado*
club or bar hop in lively
Bairro Alto.

Day 2

Mountain splendour

Either meander some more around Porto or Coimbra,
or hire a car and take a trip east into the wild
countryside of Parque Natural da Serra da Estrela,
where you can discover – on foot, by bike, or on
horseback – this rugged national park.

Day 6

Star of the Alentejo

Strike out 130km (80 miles) east of Lisbon to reach Évora, capital of the Alentejo and the region's most spectacular town. The old town is a lovely place just to wander, but you can also see impressive Roman ruins, visit beautiful churches, feast on Alentejan cuisine, and wine-taste in the surrounding hills.

Day 8

On the beach

Depending on the time of year, you can lounge or take a walk on Lagos' fabulous beaches, backed by gold and russet-streaked cliffs. Tavira also has some amazing sands, a short ferry ride away on the Ilha de Tavira. Fitness fans might try some water sports or a round of golf before the flight home from Faro.

Day 5

Sintra

Remain in Lisbon and see the sights, or spend a peaceful day in magical Sintra, which spills across lush hills 31km (19 miles) northwest of the capital. Wonder at its spectacular monuments and enjoy an evening meal at one of town's excellent restaurants. (see page 150).

Day 7

Algarve towns

Linger a little longer in Évora before heading farther south in the afternoon. Recommended Algarve towns are either vibrantly pretty Lagos, or elegant, graceful Tavira. Both places have interesting historic centres, so whichever you choose will reward a wander.

CONTENTS

🎯 FEATURES

INTRODUCTION

Few countries have risen as triumphantly or fallen as for-lornly as Portugal. From pre-eminent global superpower in the 16th century, with far-flung colonies and abundant riches, to brushed-off backwater of Continental Europe, Portugal is again an optimistic country and society in transition.

STRONG TRADITIONS AND NEW HORIZONS

Portugal has raced to catch up with its neighbours in the EU. Parts of the country are suddenly modern and cosmopolitan, while much remains stubbornly traditional. Visitors will find stunning architecture and fashions in Lisbon and Porto along-side women decked out head to toe in traditional dress. In more remote parts of the country, families still trudge along behind wooden oxcarts.

Portugal's history has left an inescapable imprint on both the land and people. The Phoenicians came to trade, Romans constructed roads and cities, Jews were physicians, artisans and mapmakers, and the Moors left great citadels, almond orchards and whitewashed villages of labyrinthine alleyways. The inhabitants of the northern regions reveal Germanic and Celtic origins in their blue eyes and fair skin, while the dark eyes and olive complexions of the Moors and their plaintive style of singing can still be seen and heard in the south.

PORTUGAL'S TREASURES

Today, travellers are discovering more of the varied treasures of Portugal, even though most stick to the sunny beaches of the Algarve or the sophisticated city life of the capital, Lisbon. Though Portugal's most celebrated destinations are among the highlights of Europe, those willing to venture beyond will be richly rewarded. Portugal – less than half the area of Britain and home to just 10.3 million people – has hundreds of unique attractions, is surprisingly easy to explore and offers an astounding variety of landscapes within relative proximity.

Scenic Almourol Castle

Rebuilt after the devastating earthquake of 1755, Lisbon has spectacular vistas and delightful areas that reflect its Moorish roots. The city straddles seven hills and overlooks the Tagus, or Tejo, the river that flows from Spain through central Portugal.

With about 160km (100 miles) of coastline, the Algarve is one of Europe's premier beach destinations. Its abundant sports, beaches, hospitable weather and easily organised package holidays attract as many visitors as the rest of Portugal combined. The blocks of tourist apartments and hotels are atypical for the country, but the coast remains true to its hype. Sun-seekers venture south for the golden sands, secluded coves in ochre-coloured rock formations and deep blue waters.

North of the Algarve lie the agricultural plains of the sun-scorched Alentejo and the Roman city of Évora; and stretching to the Spanish border are clifftop castles, small whitewashed villages and fields of wheat, olives and cork oaks.

The regions Estremadura and Ribatejo extend north of Lisbon along the Atlantic and into the central plains. It is a land of coastal fishing villages, beaches, agricultural towns hugging the Tagus River and grand religious monuments, such as the Alcobaça and Batalha abbeys, the famed shrine at Fátima and the Convento de Cristo in Tomar, as well as the impressive castle-topped town of Óbidos.

Further north is the varied landscape of the Beiras, a land of forests, the Serra da Estrela mountain range (the country's highest and where the famous Serra cheese comes from), picturesque fortified towns, coastal lagoons and the university in Coimbra, Portugal's great intellectual centre and one of the oldest universities in Europe.

⦿ CASTLES GREAT AND SMALL

Rooted across its landscape, Portugal has a rich heritage of nearly 200 medieval castles. Some grew from Roman forts, others from fortified villages. The Moors' presence is still strong in Lisbon's São Jorge castle and in the hilltop ruins above Sintra. Most were built by Portuguese kings concerned with defending the land from coastal invasion or from neighbouring Spain. Much the busiest builder was Dinis, son of Afonso III, who became king in 1279 and built or rebuilt one castle after another until his death in 1325. Frontier fortifications rose from Alcoutim on the Guadiana River to Valença on the Minho. Sturdy keeps stand, such as the one at Beja in the Alentejo. Gorgeous castles pose in solitary splendour, like Almourol on a river island near Tomar. Castles in Estremoz, Óbidos, Palmela, Setúbal, Almeida and elsewhere have been transformed into *pousadas*, splendid hotels with dramatic views.

The far north looks and feels very different from southern and central Portugal. It is lush, green and starkly traditional. The Douro Valley is dotted with magnificent terraced vineyards that produce grapes for the country's centuries-old port wine. The wine is shipped from river-hugging *quintas* (estates) to cellars in Vila Nova de Gaia, across the river from Porto, Portugal's second largest city. Once mainly an industrial, workmanlike city, Porto now claims a revitalised cultural scene and is fascinating in its own right.

Portugal's Atlantic beaches attract surfers from all over the world

The Minho, north of Porto, includes the ancient state of Portucale. The region, perhaps Portugal's most beautiful, contains the lush Peneda-Gerês National Park and some historic gems, such as the towns of Guimarães (where Portugal was born), Braga and Viana do Castelo, a popular coastal resort.

Tucked away in the northeastern corner is Portugal's most remote and perhaps most unusual region: Trás-os-Montes (literally 'beyond the mountains'). In this land long reputed to be the haunt of witches and wolves, traditional mores continue much as they have for centuries. The sparsely populated region especially appeals to hikers, who come to explore beautiful parks, wild moorlands, isolated villages and stout citadels in towns like Bragança and Chaves.

WHEN TO GO AND WHAT TO DO

When to go and how long to stay largely depends on your own interests. January, when the Algarve is particularly beautiful with almond trees in blossom, it is usually sunny and dry, though a chill is not unknown. Spring and autumn are wonderful times to be anywhere in Portugal. July and August can be hot and crowded in Lisbon and popular resorts, but temperate in the north. Winters are mild except in the far north which can be cold and wet.

Magnificent year-round weather has transformed parts of Portugal, particularly the Algarve, into a huge destination for sporting holidays. Superb golf facilities abound and horse-riding, tennis, game fishing, sailing and windsurfing are immensely popular. Stunning beaches can be found all along the coast though the water can be cold up north. Along the west coast are a number of spots offering fine sport fishing and world-class surfing.

Portugal has plenty of exuberant local festivals and street markets when whole villages come to life. More sophisticated affairs – hip nightclubs, cosmopolitan restaurants and lively bars – can be found in the larger cities.

This part of the world, at the western edge of Europe, is best discovered at an unhurried pace. One of the great joys is enjoying Portuguese cuisine and wine, whether at a simple country inn or a chic new spot in Lisbon or Porto. Predictably, local cooking owes much to the country's close ties to the sea. Many people are familiar with Portugal's famed port wines from the north, but a great secret is the affordable and unpretentious table wines of Alentejo, Dão and Douro – it's great fun to go tasting both at glorious rural vineyards or city cellars.

While Portugal undoubtedly looks to the future, happily, the beauty of its landscape, its rich architectural heritage, as well as the national warmth and hospitality, all remain comfortingly constant.

A BRIEF HISTORY

The early history of Portugal is closely related to that of the entire Iberian peninsula. Prehistoric cultures flourished first in the north and in today's Alentejo region of south-central Portugal. The south was visited by a number of peoples who came primarily to trade, including the Phoenicians, the Mycenaean Greeks and the Carthaginians. The Phoenicians established a trading post at Lisbon around 1200BC, calling it either Alis Ubbo or Olissipo. When Celtic peoples crossed the Pyrenees in the first millennium BC, they intermarried with the existing Iberian population and built a series of hilltop fort communities or *citânias*, the finest example of which is at Briteiros (see page 81).

The Carthaginians, under Hannibal, recruited locals to fight as mercenaries against Rome. The Romans eventually defeated them and invaded the Iberian peninsula. Their occupation was fiercely opposed by the Lusitani, who were Celts living in central Portugal. The Lusitanian leader, Viriato, kept the Roman forces at bay until he was betrayed and assassinated in 139BC.

The Romans cultivated grapes, wheat and olives, built roads and bequeathed the Latin foundations of the

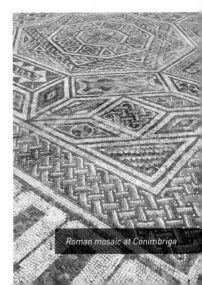

Roman mosaic at Conimbriga

12

Moorish doorway in Silves

Portuguese language and a strong base of Christian belief. Julius Caesar founded many cities, including Ebora (Évora), where the remains of a Roman temple survive (see page 97), and Pax Julia (Beja). Lisbon – Olissipo – he renamed Felicitas Julia. It became the Romans' western capital.

THE MOORS AND THE RECONQUEST

In AD711 a great Muslim invasion fleet from North Africa crossed the Strait of Gibraltar. In a matter of only a few years, the Moors had conquered almost all of Iberia, except for the small Christian kingdom of Asturias in northern Spain. Lisbon became a thriving outpost under Muslim occupation.

The Moors failed to penetrate much further north than Aveiro about halfway up the Atlantic Coast. They settled in the Alentejo, along the Tagus river and in the Algarve (which they named *al-Gharb*, or 'Western Land'). By the mid-ninth century, al-Gharb had become a Moorish kingdom, with a capital at Chelb, or Silves (see page 114).

The Moors introduced new crops, including oranges and rice, to the region. Their highly distinctive whitewashed houses and filigree chimneys are features of Portugal to this day, as are *azulejos* (handpainted, glazed ceramic tiles). Many Moorish place names also survive, including that of Fátima, the pre-eminent Catholic site in Portugal. Unlike their successors, the Moors were tolerant of the many different peoples who lived together in Portugal, including Berbers, Arabs, Christians and Jews. Even so, they were regarded as an occupying power by the local Christian population, who started the Christian Reconquest, to drive out the Muslims.

It was not until 1128, when Dom Afonso Henriques became the Count of Portucale, that the struggle to regain power met with any real success. Henriques consolidated his position by defeating the Moors at the Battle of Ourique in 1139, and celebrated by naming himself the first king of Portugal. In 1147, with the help of assorted Crusaders, he forced the Moors from their citadel in Lisbon. By 1185, the frontier between Christianity and Islam had been drawn south of the Tagus. In 1249, King Afonso III (1248–1279) finally completed the Reconquest and secured borders for Portugal – 250 years before the Spanish could do the same.

CONSOLIDATION AND GOLDEN AGE

Afonso III moved his capital from Coimbra to Lisbon in 1260, six years after he had called the first *Cortes* (parliament) in Leiria. His successor, Dom Dinis (1279–1325), consolidated Portugal's borders by constructing castles along the frontier with Castile.

The last of the Afonsin dynasty, King Fernando I (1367–1383), formed an alliance with the English against Spain. When Fernando died without an heir, the Spanish claimed the throne through marriage between the two royal houses. Spain was backed by Portuguese aristocrats, eager to avoid war.

The army of Juan I of Castile invaded Portugal in 1383, but João of Avis, recently proclaimed King João I of Portugal, defeated the Spaniards in a decisive battle fought in 1385 at Aljubarrota, about 100km (62 miles) north of Lisbon. Batalha Monastery (see page 48) was built in gratitude. The victory secured independence

Map in Coimbra showing Portuguese discovery voyages

from Spain. A new alliance with England was sealed in the 1386 Treaty of Windsor; a year later João of Avis married Philippa of Lancaster, the daughter of John of Gaunt. Their third surviving son, the Duke of Viseu, Master of the Order of Christ, would change the map of the world – he was Henry the Navigator.

BUILDING AN EMPIRE

Because Portugal faced the Atlantic Ocean rather than the Mediterranean Sea, it remained cut off from most trade routes. However, in the 15th century, when the Ottoman Turks dominated the Mediterranean, shipbuilding technology began to improve. Longer Atlantic journeys became a serious prospect, particularly after peace with Spain in 1411, and Portugal began to seek overseas conquests.

Prince Henry, the Navigator, retired to what was known as the 'end-of-the-world', the Sagres peninsula in the Algarve (see page 109). There he established a centre of research that attracted astronomers, cartographers and other leading scientists of the day. Henry established expeditions that ultimately succeeded in redefining Europeans' understanding of the world. During his lifetime, Portuguese caravels sailed far beyond the westernmost point of Africa. With the colonisation of Madeira and the Azores, the foundations were laid for the future Portuguese empire. The Portuguese also sailed down the west coast of Africa, going beyond Cape Bojador in 1434, a feat until then considered to be impossible.

Henry died in 1460, but Portugal's discovery voyages continued. The king who ruled over the golden age of exploration

⊘ GREAT EXPLORATIONS

Portugal's maritime explorations changed the world. Spurred on by Prince Henry the Navigator (who never went further than north Africa), the Portuguese were the first Europeans to sail into the Atlantic and down the coast of Africa, and the first – in a fleet commanded by Vasco da Gama – to reach India by sea from the west. They were the first Europeans to reach Ceylon, Sumatra, the spice islands of the Moluccas, and the first to trade with China and Japan. To the west, the Portuguese were the first to set foot in South America, discovering Brazil. In fact, there are clues that the Portuguese reached the North American coast well before the 1492 Christopher Columbus voyage to the Caribbean.

A Portuguese, Fernão de Magalhães – Magellan – led the first, Spanish-sponsored, circumnavigation of the world, though he did not survive it. Portuguese seamanship was widely respected; England's Francis Drake employed a Portuguese pilot on his Golden Hind voyage.

– and exploitation – was Manuel I 'The Fortunate' (1495–1521). The many discoveries made during his reign would assure his position as Europe's richest ruler. He could well afford to erect monuments as elegant as the Tower of Belém and as impressive as Lisbon's Jerónimos Monastery.

⊘ MANUELINE ARCHITECTURE

The Portuguese may be principally known for *azulejo* designs and port wine, but equally important is the ornate style of architecture and stone carving that suddenly appeared in Portugal in the late 15th century. It flourished for only a few decades, for the most part coinciding with the reign of Manuel I (1495–1521), for which it was christened 'Manueline.'

Probably triggered by the great ocean voyages of discovery, it took late Gothic as a base and added fanciful decoration, dramatic touches that were frequent references to the sea. Stone was carved like knotted rope and sculpted into imitation coral, seahorses, nets and waves, as well as non-nautical designs. The style first appeared in the small Igreja de Jesus in Setúbal (see page 44) and Lisbon's Torre de Belém (see page 37) and Mosteiro dos Jerónimos (see page 37). The style reached a peak of complexity in the unfinished chapels of the monastery at Batalha (see page 48).

You can also see exuberant Manueline stonework all over the Algarve; look for the church portals and windows at Silves (the Igreja da Misericórdia), Alvor and particularly at Monchique. In the 16th century, the style fell out of favour and, by 1540, Portugal had joined with the rest of Europe, building in the more sober Renaissance style.

The architecture that eased Portugal from Gothic into Renaissance still bears his name: the Manueline style is whimsically flamboyant and decorative, and rife with references to the sea. The most significant expedition under Manuel's flag was Vasco da Gama's legendary sea voyage from Lisbon in the summer of 1497 – immortalised in *The Lusiads* (1572), the epic poem by Portugal's national poet, Luís de Camões

Mosteiro dos Jerónimos, a fine example of Manueline architecture

(1524–1580). Rounding what is now known as the Cape of Good Hope, da Gama found what Columbus had been searching for in 1492 (although in the wrong direction): the sea route to the lucrative spices of the East. The Portuguese thus ended the Venetian monopoly on Eastern trade and began attracting merchants from all over Europe to Lisbon.

Portugal and Spain, the planet's foremost maritime powers, agreed to divide the world between them by means of the 1494 Treaty of Tordesillas. This accorded everything lying more than 370 leagues west of the Cape Verde Islands to Spain, while everything lying to the east went to Portugal, thus giving Portugal a free hand in exploiting the Orient. In 1500, Portuguese explorer Pedro Álvares Cabral came upon Brazil.

Trading posts were set up along the west and east coasts of Africa, in the Middle East (Hormuz), southern India (Goa), Malaysia (Malacca) and even in China (Macau). Profits came primarily from trading in eastern spices, silk and porcelain, African gold and slaves, as well as through importing copious amounts of sugar from Brazil and São Tomé.

Wealth helped disguise inherent weaknesses in the Portuguese state. No entrepreneurial class developed, as it did in Holland and England. The only real entrepreneurs were Jews, who were forced either to embrace Christianity or face expulsion. The Inquisition took root in the 1530s, and the Counter-Reformationary Jesuit order gained control of education in Portugal during the 1560s. The new colonies encouraged emigration and the population was soon depleted. When the king (and cardinal) Dom Henrique died leaving no heir in 1580, King Philip II of Spain marched in and, backed by wealthy Portuguese, forced the union of the two crowns.

SPANISH RULE AND RESTORATION

Philip II of Spain became Filipe I of Portugal in 1581 but he upheld Portuguese autonomy, making no attempt to unite his two kingdoms. It took 60 years for the Portuguese to organise a successful uprising against the occupation. On 1 December 1640 – a date still celebrated as Portugal's Restoration Day – Spanish rule was finally overthrown. The Duke of Bragança was crowned King João IV in a festive ceremony that took place on Lisbon's beautiful riverfront square, the Terreiro do Paço (today the Praça do Comércio).

His grandson, João V, enjoyed a long and glittering reign (1706–1750). As

Voador

On 7 October 1709 a Jesuit named Bartolomeu Gusmão showed King João V a flying machine he had invented – an aerostat called Passarola (Big Bird). An amazed public called him Voador (Flyer), but the king, uninterested, did not encourage Gusmão's ideas on aerial navigation.

money poured in from gold discoveries in Brazil, the king spent it on lavish monuments and buildings (including the aqueduct that still brings fresh water into the centre of Lisbon). However, it was Portugal's citizens, overburdened with taxes, who bore the brunt of the king's extravagances.

Azulejo showing Lisbon's royal palace before the earthquake

DESTRUCTION, REBUILDING AND THE PENINSULAR WAR

The middle of the 18th century marks a great divide between early history and modern times in Portugal. On All Saints' Day, 1 November 1755, as crowds packed the churches to honour the dead, Lisbon and parts of Portugal all the way to the Algarve were devastated by one of the worst earthquakes ever recorded. Churches crumbled and fires spread through the city. Between 15,000 and 60,000 people were thought to have died.

The task of rebuilding fell to the power behind the throne, an ambitious and tyrannical government minister, Sebastião José de Carvalho e Melo, who is more usually remembered as the Marquês de Pombal. Pombal dominated Portugal as an enlightened despot, banishing the Jesuits and executing members of the nobility accused of being involved in an assassination attempt on the king. He abolished slavery, reformed education and diversified Portuguese trade. Although he eventually lost his hold on power shortly after King José's death in 1777, many of Pombal's

António de Oliveira Salazar

reforms survived, laying the foundation for the modern Portuguese state.

At the beginning of the 19th century, Napoleon managed to drag Portugal into the heat of Europe's conflicts. France invaded in 1807 when Portugal refused to close its ports to British shipping. The royal family fled to Brazil and the British general, Arthur Wellesley (later the Duke of Wellington), countered the invasions. The final battle came in 1810–1811, when the French, unable to pass the fortifications at Torres Vedras, retreated back to Spain.

THE FALL OF THE MONARCHY

In 1814, Portugal made peace with France and Brazil was raised to the status of a full kingdom the following year. Portugal itself was ruled as a virtual British protectorate. A military coup in 1820 finally persuaded João VI to return to Portugal in 1821 and agree to a new constitution.

Peace proved elusive, though, and the country was again torn by war – this time pitting brother against brother. Pedro IV, previously Emperor of Brazil (which had asserted its independence from Portugal), fought to wrest the crown from Miguel I, his absolutist brother. Pedro won, though he died of consumption only months later at the age of 36. His adolescent daughter, Maria da Glória, assumed the throne.

Widespread discontent arose from continued government instability, futile attempts to modernise the economy and coffers depleted from the cost of maintaining overseas colonies. Republican idealists led a failed coup in 1891. The government declared itself bankrupt in 1892 and emigration reached unprecedented levels. Finally, in 1908, King Carlos and his eldest son, Luís Filipe, were assassinated as they rode in an open carriage through the Praça do Comércio in Lisbon. The younger son survived to become King Manuel II, but he was deposed two years later and forced to flee to Britain, thus ending more than 750 years of monarchy.

THE REPUBLIC AND THE NEW STATE

The new republic was unable to provide the stability Portugal needed. Governments changed no fewer than 45 times between 1910 and 1926, and the country's disastrous involvement in World War I led to economic chaos. After a revolution in 1926, General António Óscar Carmona assumed control, two years later entrusting the economy to António de Oliveira Salazar, an economics professor at Coimbra University. His skills were basic yet the exhausted Portuguese finances soon began to improve. In 1932, Salazar was named prime minister. His austere, authoritarian regime – the *Estado Novo* (New State) – favoured economic progress and nationalism. He kept Portugal neutral in World War II, but permitted the Allies to use the Azores as a base.

TOWARD THE PRESENT

Salazar's New State began to unravel when Portugal's former colonies demanded independence. In 1974, soldiers carrying red carnations in their rifle barrels successfully deposed the government in a peaceful coup that came to be known as the 'Carnation Revolution'. Portugal then disengaged itself from

Mozambique and Angola and the country absorbed the million or so refugees who fled to a motherland most had never seen.

Portugal suffered several years of political confusion, but stable democracy finally took hold. With its entry into the European Community (EU) in 1986, the pace of development quickened. EU aid made Portugal one of the fastest-growing countries in Europe, and the escudo was abandoned in favour of the euro.

Portugal won its first Nobel prize in many years when the Nobel Prize for Literature was awarded in 1998 to José Saramago. That year also saw Portugal host the World Expo, and in 2001 Porto was named European Capital of Culture.

Hosting the 2004 UEFA European Football Championship and reaching the final put the country at the centre of the world stage.

Portugal's government has seesawed between Socialists and Social Democrats. In 2005, Jóse Sócrates was elected prime minister – the first absolute majority for the Socialists since 1974 – and a former Social Democrat prime minister, Cavaco Silva, was elected president in 2006 and again in 2011.

The financial crisis of 2008 caused Portugal's budget deficit to explode and Sócrates was forced to ask the EU and IMF for a 78-billion euro bailout package and announce early elections in 2011. Those elections were won by the Social Democrats, led by Pedro Passos Coelho who became prime minister. Harsh austerity measures helped reduce the budget deficit, restore a fragile economic growth and exit the bailout programme in 2014.

However, this didn't stop more than 100,000 Portuguese emigrating to the former colonies of Brasil, Angola or Mozambique with their booming economies. Many have returned in recent years as the economic revival took root and unemployment fell to its lowest level in a decade under the current prime minister, António Costa, leader of the socialist party, who was sworn in following the 2015 elections.

LANDMARKS

200BC Carthaginians began regular visits.

147–139BC Lusitanian hero Viriato resists Roman invasion.

50BC Julius Caesar makes Olissipo (Lisbon) Rome's western capital.

4th century AD Christianity makes its mark.

711 Moors from Africa begin 500-year occupation.

10th century Portucale is recognised in the north.

1139–85 Afonso Henriques rules as Portugal's first king.

1249 The Moors are expelled from the Algarve.

1255 King Afonso III transfers capital from Coimbra to Lisbon.

1385 Battle of Ajubarrota; Portuguese defeat Castilians; João I is king.

1386 Treaty of Windsor; João I marries Philippa of Lancaster.

1415 Discovery of Madeira followed by the Azores in 1427.

1494 Treaty of Tordesillas: the world divided by Portugal and Spain.

1497–8 Vasco da Gama opens sea route to India.

1500 Pedro Álvares Cabral discovers Brazil.

1580–1640 Portugal falls under rule of Spain.

1755 The Great Earthquake destroys Lisbon.

1808 The Peninsular War; Sir Arthur Wellesley leads British forces.

1822 Brazil proclaims independence.

1910 Monarchy falls; Portugal becomes a Republic.

1926 Military coup paves way to Salazar's long dictatorship.

1970 Salazar dies; Marcelo Caetano becomes prime minister.

1974 'Carnation Revolution'; Socialist Mário Soares becomes prime minister.

1986 Portugal, with Spain, enters the European Community (now EU).

2002 The euro becomes official currency.

2004 Euro championship held throughout the country.

2011 Portugal is granted a 78-billion euro bailout package.

2014 End of bailout programme, beginning of the slow economic recovery.

2015 Socialist António Costa becomes prime minister.

2016 Social democrat Marcelo Rebelo de Sousa becomes the new president. Portuguese national football team wins Euro 2016 tournament in France.

2017 Wildfires ravage the country killing over 100 people in four months.

*Mosteiro de Santa Maria de Alcobaça,
the largest church in Portugal*

WHERE TO GO

Although a small country, Portugal is blessed with incredible geographical diversity. Occupying the western sixth of the Iberian peninsula, the country has good communications and is easy to explore. Even a relatively short amount of time and distance covered allows you to sample varied regions and attractions, including famed beaches, rugged mountains, splendid castles, traditional rural villages and gorgeous medieval cities. Most visitors still focus on the appealing capital, Lisbon, and the alluring sunny beaches of the Algarve, but there's much more to Portugal.

LISBON

For years, **Lisbon ❶** has enjoyed a reputation as a relatively quiet town, without the hustle, bustle and general hassle of other major European cities. While there are still ample remnants of that easy-going charm, the gap is quickly closing; the city now has its fair share of traffic and noise.

Portugal's capital city is the country's largest, with a population of more than 2 million (in the metropolitan area). Due to a massive earthquake that obliterated much of the ancient city, most of the architecture that remains is from the 18th century. However, older sections of the town survive in the winding alleys of the medieval and Moorish district, known as the Alfama.

Alfama by tram

Trams are the best ways to get up into Alfama: No. 12 goes from Praça da Figueira, No. 28 from Bairro Alto. Tram 15 plies the waterfront to Belém from Praça do Comércio.

The rooftops of Alfama

The centre of Lisbon is small, compact and easy to get around. The city is built on hills – by legend seven, but in fact more – providing several splendid vantage points. Perhaps the best place to start your tour of Lisbon is from the Moors' old castle, the **Castelo de São Jorge** (St George's Castle; daily summer 9am–9pm, winter 9am–6pm; www.castelodesaojorge. pt). The fall of the castle to Afonso Henriques, Portugal's first king, and a rough bunch of crusaders in 1147 proved crucial in the Reconquest of Portugal from the Moors. From its ramparts you can take in the whole of the city and the broad Rio Tejo (River Tagus), spanned by what in 1966, when it was completed, was the longest suspension bridge in Europe.

ALFAMA AND BAIXA

The atmospheric medieval **Alfama** Ⓐ *bairro* (district) is Lisbon's most picturesque and fascinating area and was one of the few areas to survive the 1755 earthquake. A legacy of the Moors, it spills down the side of a hill between the Castelo de São Jorge and the Tagus with all the colour of an Arabian bazaar: a labyrinth of crooked streets, cobbled alleyways, decaying old houses and palaces, fish stalls and *fado* music clubs (see page 131).

Another majestic view of the city is from a lovely park, **Miradouro de Santa Luzia**, just down the hill from the castle.

Lisbon's **Sé Patriarcal** (cathedral; daily 9am–7pm, until 6pm in winter; free) appears out of nowhere at a bend in the road. Begun as a fortress-church in the 12th century, its towers and walls suggest a beleaguered citadel. Adjacent to the cathedral is the lovely **Igreja de Santo António da Sé**, named after Lisbon's most cherished saint, St Anthony of Padua.

Just beyond the Alfama is the church honouring Lisbon's patron saint **São Vicente de Fora** (St Vincent Beyond the Walls; Tue–Fri 9am–4pm, Sat until 6pm, Sun until 1pm), an Italianate church and monastic cloister. The latter is the true highlight: its courtyards are lined with blue-and-white *azulejos* and the views from the roof are among the best in the city.

Down towards the river is the **Museu Nacional do Azulejo** Ⓑ (National Azulejo Museum; Tue–Sun 10am–6pm; free on Sun until 2pm; www.museudoazulejo.gov.pt), devoted entirely to the art of painted and glazed ceramic tiles, a national art form. About 12,000 are on display here, from 15th-century polychrome designs to 20th-century art deco styles. A prized possession is

⊙ ST VINCENT OF LISBON

The remains of St Vincent are kept in a beautiful silver reliquary at São Vicente de Fora. Vincent was martyred at Valencia in 336, but when the Moors took that city in the 8th century the inhabitants fled by sea, taking the relics of St Vincent with them. They were driven ashore on the coast of Algarve at the cape now known as Cape St Vincent, and there they remained until Dom Afonso Henriques had them brought to the capital and deposited in the church he had just built. Two ravens faithfully escorted the saintly relics, which explains why many a Lisbon lamppost bears the symbol of a sailing ship with a bird fore and aft.

Lisbon's cathedral

the *Lisbon Panorama*, a 36m (118ft) long tile composition of Lisbon's riverside as it looked before the 1755 earthquake. Part of the museum, which occupies a former convent, is the fabulous interior of the small church of **Igreja da Madre de Deus**, a mix of gilt rococo and beautiful *azulejos*.

A district known as the **Baixa** Ⓒ (Lower City) – the low-lying area between hills on either side – was devastated by the earthquake. The Marquês de Pombal supervised the city's reconstruction, redesigning it to a geometric grid of broad avenues. The building style came to be known as 'Pombaline'.

The Baixa is Lisbon's principal business district. **Praça do Comércio**, a grand square with a vast triumphal arch, is lined on three sides by gracious arcaded buildings. The square has seen its share of watershed political events: King Carlos and his son were felled by an assassin's bullets here in 1908, and it was the site of one of the first uprisings of the Carnation Revolution of 1974. The **Lisboa Welcome** city information centre is on the west side of the square. Nearby, an interesting **Design and Fashion Museum** (Rua Augusta 24, currently closed for renovation; www.mude.pt) boasts over 2,000 pieces by famous names such as Jean-Paul Gaultier, Vivienne Westwood and Yves Saint-Laurent.

Ferries cross the Tagus from a point near the square and from another to the west near the **Cais do Sodré** railway station, where trains depart for Estoril and Cascais. Not far, on Avenida 24 de Julho 50 is the **Mercado da Ribeira**, the city's main food market (Mon–Sat 6am–2pm) offering not only fresh seafood and vegetables but also an excellent food court (Sun–Wed 10am–midnight and Thu–Sat 10–2am) as well as antique and craft market at weekends.

A wide pedestrian shopping street, **Rua Augusta**, leads from the Praça do Comércio through a stately arch to the central square of Lisbon, Praça Dom Pedro IV, better known as the **Rossio**. Once the scene of bullfights, it is now a popular meeting point, ringed by cafés. The National Theatre is on the north side, and across the road is the **Estação do Rossio** (with trains to Sintra and Queluz), which looks like a Moorish palace with horseshoe arches. To the north another lively square, **Praça dos**

Praça do Comércio

Restauradores, has an obelisk commemorating the overthrow of Spanish rule in Portugal in 1640. The main **Portuguese tourist office** is at Palácio Foz, on the west side of the square.

The broad, leafy Avenida da Liberdade runs for 1km (0.6 mile) north, flanked by gardens, ponds and fountains, as far as the Praça Marquês de Pombal (the Rotunda), where a statue of the autocratic statesman Pombal gazes over the city and, at times, over crowds celebrating football victories.

North of Parque Eduardo VII, off Avenida António Augusto Aguiar, is **Museu Gulbenkian** Ⓓ (Wed–Mon 10am–6pm; www. museu.gulbenkian.pt), Lisbon's most remarkable museum. One of the best private collections of fine art in Europe (bequeathed to Portugal), it was created as an exhibition space for the thousands of works of art acquired by the Armenian-born billionaire Calouste Gulbenkian. His spectacular collection of fine art and vast personal wealth brought Portugal more than a museum. From the philanthropic foundation created in his name came concert and exhibition halls, a symphony orchestra, a ballet company and choral groups and libraries. Gulbenkian funds have also provided equipment for hospitals and social services, rehabilitation centres for the handicapped, grants and subsidies to restore buildings as well as bursaries to struggling artists. From his home in Paris, Gulbenkian came to Portugal in 1942 to escape Nazi domination in World War II and became fond of the country and its people. He died in Portugal in 1955 aged 86.

A little further north you'll find the impressive 18th-century **Aguas Livres Aqueduct**, which still carries water along its 18km (11-mile) length.

BAIRRO ALTO

Back toward the river and just west of the Praça do Comércio is **Lapa**, an elegant residential neighbourhood. Its oustanding attraction is the **Museu Nacional de Arte Antiga ⑤** (National Museum of Ancient Art; Tue–Sun 10am–6pm; www.museu dearteantiga.pt), Portugal's largest museum. Among its masterpieces are *The Adoration of St Vincent*, a multi-panel work attributed to the 15th-century Portuguese master, Nuno Gonçalves, and *The Temptation of St Anthony*, a fantastic hallucination by Hieronymus Bosch.

The **Bairro Alto** (Upper City) is a hilly area of captivating houses decorated with wrought-iron balconies, birdcages and flowerpots. At night it is loaded with atmosphere from numerous restaurants, bars and *fado* houses.

Perched on the edge of the Bairro Alto is one of Lisbon's most evocative sights, the shell of the 14th-century **Igreja do Carmo** (Carmelite Church), which was packed with worshippers on All Saints' Day, 1755, when the terrible earthquake brought the roof down. The church remains preserved as an atmospheric ruin and contains a small archaeology museum. Nearby, the sumptuous 16th-century **Igreja de São Roque** contains a lavish baroque chapel of São João Baptista (St John the Baptist) and a small museum of sacred art.

You can easily walk to the Bairro Alto from the central squares in the Baixa, but it's fun to go by tram. You can also reach the Bairro Alto

Igreja do Carmo

from the 30m (98ft) **Elevador de Santa Justa** (for hours, check www.carris.pt) just off Rossio square. The stately elevator that takes you to a viewing platform is a 1902 marvel of iron and glass, built by Raul Mesnier de Ponsard, almost certainly inspired by Gustave Eiffel. At the top, steps behind the lift lead to the upper Rua do Carmo. The route back downhill meanders through the elegant shopping area of **Chiado**, totally rebuilt, after a fire swept through the district in 1988.

The Bairro Alto reveals Lisbon at its most quixotic and colourful. Once the tawdry haunt of prostitutes, today it is cleaner – apart from the occasional daubs of graffiti – well lit and the place to find independent bookshops (*livrarias*), small grocery shops, delightful restaurants, bars and *fado* houses. When night falls, Bairro Alto becomes Lisbon's liveliest district and the city's partygoers fill the narrow lanes until it's time to go clubbing.

Quite different, with tasteful design and comfortable easy chairs, is the elegant port wine-tasting establishment, **Lisboa Solar** – run by **Instituto dos Vinhos do Douro e Porto** (Douro Wines and Port Institute; Mon–Fri 11am–midnight, Sat 3pm–midnight; www.ivdp.pt) in Rua de São Pedro de Alcântara. It is opposite the top of **Elevador da Glória**, which links Restauradores in the Baixa to the upper city and the Elevador de Santa Justa. Both *elevadores* confirm the artful eccentricity of the area, and if Eiffel is no longer credited with building the Santa Justa funicular, his engineering skills are unquestioned in Porto's bridges and others in the north, galleries in Lisbon's Sociedade de Geografia and even a garage in Rua Alexandre Herculano.

BELÉM

Some 6km (4 miles) west of Praça do Comércio lies the riverside district of Belém. Many of the great voyages of discovery set out from here in the 15th and 16th centuries. The new sea routes produced a golden age of commerce, and King Manuel built two magnificent monuments to commemorate the country's achievements.

One is the **Torre de Belém** ❻ (Tue–Sun 10am–5.30pm, summer until 6.30pm; www.torrebelem.gov.pt), a small but exquisitely romantic medieval fortress (particularly when floodlit by night) erected in 1515 to defend the entry to Lisbon and one of the finest examples of Manueline architecture.

By contrast, the majestic **Mosteiro dos Jerónimos** ❼

Puzzling poet

Fernando Pessoa (1888–1935), a sculpture of whom is seated outside the Chiado's Café A Brasileira, is esteemed as a modernist poet. Cryptic, too – he wrote under at least four names, each with a different personality.

The exquisite Torre de Belém

(Tue–Sun 10am–6.30pm, winter until 5.30pm; www.mosteiro-jeronimos.gov.pt) is Lisbon's largest religious monument and a truly formidable example of Manueline architecture. The imposing church, which has a double-decker cloister, miraculously survived the 1755 earthquake. Along with royal tombs, the monastery holds the relics of national heroes Vasco da Gama and the poet Luís de Camões. It also houses an archaeology museum. Next to it is the **Museu da Marinha** (Naval Museum; daily 10am–6pm, winter 5pm; http://ccm.marinha.pt).

Back down the street towards Lisbon is the highly popular **Museu Nacional dos Coches** (National Coach Museum; Tue–Sun 10am–6pm; http://museudoscoches.pt), located in the former riding school of the Belém Royal Palace. Across the street on the riverside stands the ultramodern, wave-like organic building of the Museum of Art, Architecture and Technology (MAAT; www.maat.pt; Wed–Mon 11am–7pm) designed by the

British architect Amanda Levete. It hosts exhibitions of contemporary artists, architects and houses the EDP Foundation's Art Collection. Other branches of the museum include the nearby Tejo Power Station and the interesting Electricity Museum.

One of Belém's best-known symbols is the modern **Padrão dos Descobrimentos** (Monument to the Discoveries; daily 10am–7pm, winter until 5.30pm; www.padraodosdescobrimentos.pt). The huge waterfront sculpture depicts Prince Henry the Navigator at the prow of a stylised caravel jutting into the River Tagus.

Other attractions in Belém include the Gulbenkian Institute's **Planetarium** and the huge **Centro Cultural de Belém** (www.ccb.pt), home to concerts and art exhibits as well as **Museo Berardo** (http://pt.museuberardo.pt; free on Sat), with one of Europe's best modern art collections including works by Warhol, Picasso and Dalí.

EASTERN LISBON

The neighbourhood designed for the World Expo '98, which replaced the faltering industrial section in the city's east, continues to draw visitors. The riverfront **Parque das Nações** (Nation's Park) is home to a world-class aquarium, the **Oceanário de Lisboa** (www.oceanario.pt). The park is easily accessed by Metro.

LISBON ENVIRONS

QUELUZ

Just 14km (8 miles) west of Lisbon is the **Palacio Nacional de Queluz** (daily 9am–6pm, longer in summer; www.parquesdes intra.pt), the sumptuous pink summer palace commissioned by Pedro III. It was built in the second half of the 18th century as an official working residence for the royal family. The

The extravagant Palácio da Pena

Palace Gardens are the pride of Queluz, with geometrically laid clipped hedges, imaginative fountains and armies of statues.

SINTRA

Though **Sintra** ❷, 30km (18 miles) to the northwest of Lisbon, suffers the effects of its enduring popularity, it is one of the finest towns in Portugal to visit. Nestling in the Serra de Sintra, it was once a coveted summer retreat for royals and today is a romantic getaway for people from all over the world. Clustered throughout the forested hillsides are old palaces and estates with spectacular vistas.

Located right in the centre of town is the spectacular **Palácio Nacional de Sintra** (daily 9.30am–6pm, longer in summer; www.parquesdesintra.pt), easily recognised by its two huge, white conical chimneys. Used since the early 14th century as a stately summer home for Portuguese kings, its interiors and furnishings are remarkable and includes one of the oldest and most valuable collections of *azulejos* to be found in Portugal.

A steep road of hairpin turns leads up into the *serra* from Sintra to the town's most spectacular monuments. The oldest is the **Castelo dos Mouros** (Moors' Castle; daily 10am–6pm, longer in summer), erected during the 8th century after the Moors occupied Portugal. The dauntless Afonso Henriques conquered it for the Christians in 1147, a major victory in the Reconquest of Portugal. Those with plenty of energy should climb the ramparts for incredible views of the forests.

On the hilltop further up the same winding road, over 450m (1,500ft) above sea level, is the **Palácio da Pena** (daily 10am–6pm, longer in summer), an outrageous architectural folly built between 1840 and 1849. The palace is an extravagant cocktail of Gothic, Renaissance, Manueline and Moorish architecture fashioned as a love nest for Queen Maria II (1834–1853) and her smitten husband, Ferdinand of Saxe-Coburg-Gotha. Inside, rooms are a riot of imaginative, ornate and, in some cases, suffocatingly sumptuous details.

English poets, writers and aesthetes visited Sintra and rhapsodised over its beauty and charm. For Lord Byron it was a 'glorious Eden'. The rich built residences exceeded

Cabo da Roca

Sailing boats aligned on the beach, Cascais

one another in odd styles – the **Quinta da Regaleira**, vast and with Gothic features, such as a mysterious initiation well, in its magical gardens; the **Quinta de Monserrate**, Moorish in style and famous for its exotic garden. The lovely **Tivoli Palácio de Seteais**, where a convention was signed after the defeat of Napoleon's forces in 1809, was created by a diamond merchant and became a luxury hotel with hand-painted walls and fine furnishings.

A short hop from Sintra are the attractive village of **Colares**, the beach at **Praia das Maçãs** and the rugged coastline at **Cabo da Roca**, the westernmost point of the European mainland. Ask for directions at Sintra's tourist office on Praça da República.

ESTORIL COAST

The Costa do Estoril begins just west of Lisbon and goes all the way around the tip of the peninsula to Guincho on the open

Atlantic. The beaches and resorts west of Lisbon are all accessible by train from the capital's Cais do Sodré station.

The palm-shaded, somewhat faded resort of **Estoril**, 24km (15 miles) from Lisbon, is famous for its casino, which inspired Ian Fleming to write *Casino Royale*.

Cascais ❸, a picturesque resort with fine beaches nearby and plenty of nightlife in summer, is as popular with day trippers from Lisbon as it is with European golfers. The **Paços do Concelho** (Town Hall) has stately windows with iron railings, separated by panels of *azulejos* depicting saints. A forbidding 17th-century fort, known as the **Cidadela** (citadel), is one of the few buildings to have survived the earthquake and tidal wave of 1755. The municipal park down the road holds the **Museu dos Condes de Castro Guimarães** (Tue–Sun 10am–1pm and 2–5pm; www.cascais.pt), a museum with archaeological remains, art works and furniture plus a flavour of the old fishing village in its fashionable heyday.

The road west (3km/2 miles from Cascais) passes **Boca do Inferno** (Mouth of Hell), a geological curiosity where, in rough weather, the waves send up astonishingly high spouts of spray accompanied by ferocious sound effects. **Guincho** is a surfers' haven 9km (6 miles) from Cascais. You have the choice of either a sandy beach or the rocks to fish from, but be careful as they face the open sea and it's often rough.

SOUTH OF THE TAGUS

The **Ponte 25 de Abril**, across the River Tagus, was the longest suspension bridge in Europe when

---

Birth of a bridge

When the Parque das Nações district rose on the Tagus riverbank east of Lisbon so did the elegant Vasco da Gama bridge stretching 17.2km (10.5 miles) across the river. It was launched on 31 March 1998 – with a banquet on the bridge.

it was opened in 1966. It leads to several destinations south of Lisbon popular with both Portuguese and international visitors.

You also might consider crossing via the newer, graceful and less congested **Vasco da Gama** bridge, which extends across the Tagus from the Parque das Naçoes to Montijo and joining the initial motorway south towards Palmela and Setúbal.

The topographical highlight of the Arrábida peninsula on the far side is undoubtedly the **Serra da Arrábida** (site of a nature reserve), a mountain chain around 35km (22 miles) long that protects the coast from the strong north winds and accounts for the Mediterranean vegetation. The tiny beach, **Portinho da Arrábida**, is popular with the Portuguese. **Setúbal ❹**, the district capital, is little more than a 20-minute drive from Lisbon by motorway, longer if you take the picturesque route via Sesimbra and Arrábida. This is olive and citrus country, with cows grazing among the trees. Setúbal is a conglomeration of market town, industrial centre, resort and Portugal's third largest fishing port.

Setúbal's greatest historical and artistic treasure, the Gothic **Igreja de Jesus**, was built around 1490 by the great French architect, Boytac, who later built Lisbon's glorious Jerónimos Monastery (see page 37). A dramatic main portal leads into the church, which has 17th-century *azulejos* on the walls, and stone pillars like twisted strands of clay.

NORTH OF LISBON

In modest Portugal, the dimensions and extravagance of the convent and palace of **Mafra** (Wed–Mon 9.30am–5.30pm; www.palaciomafra.gov.pt), 40 km (25 miles) to the northwest of Lisbon, are staggering. The riches are attributable to King João V, who in 1711 conceived this project to celebrate the long-awaited birth of his first child, Princess D. Maria, after three years of marriage. The convent took 18 years to build and employed more than 50,000 people at one time. Its huge cost gave rise to a Portuguese saying that João transformed the diamonds of Brazil into the rocks of Mafra.

The basilica has a set of six organs and two carillons of 112 bells, which are the largest in the world. The undisputed highlight of Mafra, however, is the convent library. It has a vaulted ceiling, a preciosus wood floor and shelves housing 40,000 volumes, making it the largest one-room library in Portugal.

The nature reserve and beach at Arrábida

Another 10km (6 miles) to the coast is the fishing village and growing resort of **Ericeira**, a natural port. The old section is a town of cobbled streets winding between whitewashed cottages where everything is clean, neat and treasured.

ESTREMADURA AND RIBATEJO

The historic regions north of Lisbon – Estremadura, between the River Tagus and the Atlantic coast, and Ribatejo, extending into the agricultural central plains – possess some important monuments and interesting, attractive towns.

ÓBIDOS AND THE COAST

The high medieval walls of **Óbidos** ❺ encircle a jewel of a town. It is hard to believe this inland town was once a port and coastal fortress until the sea inlet here silted up, leaving the lagoon cut off and the shoreline nearly 10km (6 miles) away.

According to tradition, the town was given as a wedding gift from King Dinis to his bride, Isabel. An entrance at the north end is guarded by the 13th-century castle, which has been converted into a luxurious *pousada*. The narrow streets inside the town's walls are enchanting, lined with whitewashed houses adorned with colourful flowers. Rua Direita, the main street, runs from one gate to the other. The parish church, **Igreja de Santa Maria**, has handsome blue 18th-century *azulejos*, an odd blue-painted ceiling and a gilded tomb in the north wall. Afonso V married his cousin, another Isabel, in this small church in 1441 when they were children (he was 10, she all of eight).

The grace and elegance of the houses within walled Óbidos might seem enough to distinguish this tiny town from most others, but it also has some important and highly rated art, particularly in its principal church, **Santa Maria** (daily Oct–Mar 9.30am–12.30pm and 2.30–5pm, Apr–Sept until 7pm). The retable of the main altar is a magnificent work by João da Costa. The Santa Catarina retable (1661) is one of several works in the town by a renowned female artist, Josefa de Óbidos (1630–84). Born in Seville to a modest painter father

Óbidos Castle is now a pousada

who moved to Portugal when she was a child, she is buried in the **Igreja de São Pedro** in Óbidos.

Due west on the coast, the old port of **Peniche** was once an island. The port's imposing fortifications were built by Spain during its period of rule in the 16th century. The fishing harbour is packed with brightly coloured, storm-battered craft and flanked by excellent informal fresh fish restaurants. The **fort** nearby held political prisoners during the Salazar régime; it is soon to be transformed into a national museum of resistance against the dictatorship. In fine weather you could take a trip to the **Ilha Berlenga**, 12km (7 miles) offshore. With an impressive 17th-century fort, the islands are now a sanctuary for seabirds.

> ### A famous daughter
>
> Josefa de Óbidos was no amateur artist but a professional who was working solidly in what was at the time a man's world. The convents were comfortable with her and much of her work was done for convent patrons. Yet her style, a blend of high baroque and provincial, brought her respect far beyond the convents. Her paintings today are not only in Óbidos churches but leading museums countrywide.

ALCOBAÇA AND BATALHA ABBEYS

Two admirable abbeys – and two of Portugal's most moving monuments – are found inland north of Óbidos. The first is the former Cistercian monastery **Mosteiro de Santa Maria de Alcobaça** (daily Oct–Mar 9am–6pm, Apr–Sep 9am–7pm; www.mosteiroalcobaca. gov.pt). Built to celebrate the victory of the 1147 battle when Dom Afonso Henriques took over the town of Santarém from the Moors, the church remains the largest in Portugal.

In the transept, about 30m (100ft) apart, are the tombs of Pedro I and Inês de Castro, their effigies facing each other and

Mosteiro da Batalha

surrounded by attendant angels. Pedro and Inês lived a tragic love story that ended with her murder – ordered by Pedro's father, King Afonso IV. Pedro, when he became king, had her long-dead body exhumed, placed on a throne and crowned. Courtiers were commanded to pay their respects to the corpse. Pedro ordered the murderers' hearts be drawn from their living bodies. The lovers' tombs are decorated with Portugal's greatest medieval stonecarving. The monastery's Cloister of Silence, ordered by King Dom Dinis in the early 14th century, is a model of harmony and simplicity.

Further north (16km/9 miles) is the even more impressive, many-turreted and buttressed **Mosteiro da Batalha** (Battle Monastery; www.mosteirobatalha.gov.pt daily Apr–Sept 9am–6.30pm, Oct–Mar 9am–6pm). King João I ordered the construction of this Gothic masterpiece in gratitude for the victory over Juan I of Castile at the Battle of Aljubarrota nearby in 1385. In the centre of the Capela do Fundador (Founder's Chapel), a tomb contains the remains of João and his queen, Philippa of Lancaster; their effigies lie side by side, hand in hand. Niches in the walls hold the tombs of their children, most notably that containing Prince Henry the Navigator.

Portugal's involvement in World War I is remembered in the monastery and two Unknown Soldiers are buried in the

Chapterhouse. This vaulted chamber, 20 sq m (65 sq ft), was a great engineering wonder in its day (around 1400). Due to fears that the unsupported ceiling would collapse at any time, the architect is said to have employed only convicts under sentence of death to work on the project.

The quintessential fishing village **Nazaré**, the Portuguese 'Nazareth', is now a thriving commercial resort and big wave surfers' mecca. However, you still might spot some elderly women in traditional dress: black shawls, bright aprons and seven petticoats (one for each day of the week).

Sítio, the 90m (300ft) cliff at the north end of Nazaré, offers an excellent vantage point over the green hilly countryside, the tiled roofs of the neatly packed town, and mile after mile of beach open to the full force of the Atlantic Ocean.

FÁTIMA

Set in bleak hill country about 135km (84 miles) north of Lisbon, **Fátima** – once just a poor village – is one of the most important centres of pilgrimage in the Catholic world, along with Lourdes in France and Santiago de Compostela in Spain.

On 13 May 1917, three young shepherds claimed they saw a series of miraculous visions of the Virgin Mary – said to have disclosed three secrets, or prophecies, to the children – followed by a solar phenomenon witnessed by thousands in October of the same year. (Two of the children died of pneumonia soon after these inexplicable events; the third, Lucia, lived as a cloistered Carmelite nun in Coimbra until her death in 2005.)

The 20th-century neo-baroque basilica that draws so many of the faithful competes in size with St Peter's in Rome. On anniversaries of the 'appearances' the great square facing the sanctuary is totally packed. In 2007 a new religious centre was opened (Mon–Fri 9am–5pm; free), named after Pope John Paul II who, although he was shot and severely injured in 1981 – the date was 13 May – credited Our Lady of Fátima with his narrow escape from the assassin's bullet. He made a pilgrimage of thanks in 1982 and personally fast-tracked the original three shepherd children towards sainthood. Pilgrimages are held on the 13th of every month.

TOMAR

Seated astride the River Nabão, **Tomar** ❻ (34km/21 miles east of Fátima) is one of Portugal's most fascinating towns. Tomar's pleasant central square, **Praça da República**, is flanked by the elegant Manueline church of São João Baptista, with an unusual octagonal belfry and intricate portico, and the 17th-century town hall. The statue in the centre of the

---

⊙ A POPULAR PILGRIMAGE

The huge Fátima sanctuary reaches peaks of devotional spectacle on 13 May and 13 October, the first and last dates in 1917 when three shepherd children saw a vision of the Virgin Mary. Before each anniversary hundreds of thousands of pilgrims make their way to Fátima, many of them on repeat visits. Initially, the Church tried to suppress accounts of the apparition and to restrain impassioned crowds. Then in 1928 the first stone of the great basilica was laid and, a year later, the cult of *Nossa Senhora da Fátima* was authorised. Now, all three children are dead and all are on their way to sainthood. So big has the Fátima phenomenon become – and the crowds – the sanctuary was extended to include a centre honouring John Paul II, which was formally opened 13 May 2007, 90 years after the first appearance of Mary to the children.

plaza tells the town's story. Beneath a colony of pigeons, it depicts Gualdim Pais, Grand Master of the Portuguese branch of the crusading Order of the Knights Templar, to whom the town was granted in 1157.

Unusual for a town so dominated by Christian crusaders, a small 15th-century **sinagoga** (synagogue; Tue–Sun 10am–1pm and 3–6pm; currently closed for renovation) sur-

The Convento do Cristo, a highlight of the Manueline style

vives on Rua Dr Joaquim Jacinto, just off the main square. The room has a high vaulted ceiling, along with eight clay pots embedded in the walls to improve the acoustics. A museum displays old Jewish tombstones.

The outstanding sights, however, are up on the hill above the town. The Templars' old stronghold, the Unesco World Heritage Sites, **Castelo dos Templários** (Templars' Castle; daily 9am–5.30pm, until 6.30 in summer; www.cm-tomar.pt) and the **Convento do Cristo** (Convent of Christ; same hours), overlook Tomar from wooded heights. Behind crenellated walls, the 12th-century convent is one of the highlights of central Portugal.

At the heart of the complex is the original Templar church, the fascinating 12th-century Charola, a 16-sided structure based on the Church of the Holy Sepulchre built over Christ's tomb in Jerusalem. Knights once attended services here on horseback. The interior is a gilded octagonal structure, which appears more pagan than Christian. A restoration has revived the Charola's esoteric paintings. The two-storey nave, added by Manuel I, is divided into an upstairs choir with a chapterhouse underneath.

One of the finest Manueline windows in Portugal is carved in the western wall of the Chapterhouse, encrusted with marine carvings. The grand Renaissance-style Claustro Principal (Great Cloister) was added in the 16th century.

Halfway up the wooded road to the Convento de Cristo is the 16th-century **Ermida da Nossa Senhora da Conceição**, a handsome little basilica in classic Italian Renaissance style.

From Tomar an enjoyable excursion is to the fairytale castle at **Almourol** (www.cm-vnbarquinha.pt), marooned on an island in the Tagus. Just upriver is **Abrantes**, with its own castle overlooking the town.

South of Tomar, the tranquil town of **Golegã** explodes every November, when the prestigious and highly enjoyable Feira Nacional do Cavalo (National Horse Fair) takes place. If you can't be here when all the horses and breeders are, at least have a look at the fine portal of the 16th-century **Igreja Matriz** and a couple of small art museums, one the remarkable **Museu de Fotografia Carlos Relvas**.

Horse fair

The Golegã horse fair (http://feiradagolega.com) in November is a great place to see Portugal's Alter horse and the light grey Lusitano, chosen by the Presidential Guard at Belém and by many keen riders for its mobility and amiable temperament.

SANTARÉM AND VILA FRANCA DE XIRA

Santarém, 78km (48 miles) northeast of Lisbon, is the ancient capital of the agricultural region of the Ribatejo, whose lifeblood is the vital River Tagus. Few of Santarém's monuments have survived, although the Jesuit

Campinos, or herdsmen, in their traditional costume

seminary and church on the main square, the triangular Largo Sá da Bandeira, has an impressive 17th-century baroque façade. North of the centre is the 15th-century **Igreja de Graça** (daily 10am–1pm and 2–6pm, winter 9.15am–12.30pm and 2–5.15pm), with a magnificent Gothic rose window, amazingly carved from a single piece of stone. To the south is the Manueline-style Marvila church (Wed–Sun 10am–noon and 2–5.30pm), with fine 17th-century *azulejos*. Across the street is an interesting archaeological museum in a beautiful Romanesque church.

A fine panoramic view can be had from the **Portas do Sol** *miradouro*, a garden surrounded by Moorish walls overlooking the River Tagus and the extensive plains of the Ribatejo. A Phoenician dye house has been found in the grounds.

In this agricultural land, bulls and horses can be seen grazing all over the Ribatejo. **Vila Franca de Xira** (45km/28 miles along the Tagus in the direction of Lisbon) is a modest town, but the centre of Portuguese bullfighting. Every July and October, a festival with Pamplona-style bull-running through the streets (called a *largada*) accompanies the bullfights. The paramount festival, lasting several days around the first Sunday in July, is called **Festas do Colete Encarnado** (Festival of the Red Waistcoat) after the gaudy costumes of the sturdy *campinos*, traditional herdsmen and horsemen. From their vivid knitted cap to tight waistcoat, three-quarter leggings and stockings, they are a spectacle in bright red, green and white. *Campinos* don their costume for every significant event and sometimes even for an ordinary day's work out on the plains.

For those more interested in birds than horses, numerous migratory species can be seen in the **Tagus Estuary Natural Reserve**, an important wetland with headquarters in **Alcochete**.

THE BEIRAS

The three ancient provinces known as the Beiras together make up the broad swathe of land lying between the Tagus and Douro rivers. Beiras means 'edge', revealing the boundary position these provinces have long occupied between northern and southern Portugal. Each of the three provinces retains its own distinctive character.

The lovely university city of Coimbra dominates the Beira Litoral (Coastal Beira). The adjacent coastline, part of the Costa de Prata (Silver Coast), has largely escaped development, though there are resorts at Figueira da Foz and Aveiro.

Inland is the spectacular terrain of the Beira Alta (Upper Beira). Small granite hills begin to develop into great mountains dressed in pine trees. The population is small and the number of tourists few, despite the strange beauty of the landscape, with giant boulders and flowery meadows. The Serra da Estrela is the backbone of the area and offers a host of wonderful

The university city of Coimbra

valleys and waterfalls for hikers, fortified by tasty regional food and the area's fabulous cheese. The Serra is also where you are likely to see Portugal's biggest endemic dog. The Serra da Estrela breed is bigger than a Labrador but has its good looks and gentle temperament. Once it was a shepherd's guard dog when wolves were a threat, now it's more likely to be a pet.

Further south, the mountains give way to the agricultural plains of the Beira Baixa (Lower Beira), which lacks the monuments and mountains of its neighbours, but still maintains an unspoiled way of life.

COIMBRA

The magnificent university city of **Coimbra** ❼, the country's capital during the 12th and 13th centuries, has been the pillar of Portuguese intellectual life since 1290. Today, it is a lively and prosperous city, brimming with students.

Igreja de Santa Cruz

The famous **Universidade de Coimbra** is the country's oldest. The university sits on top of a hill in the old town, high above the River Mondego. Wending their way up to the university are several small streets that hide *repúblicas* (halls of residence) and numerous small bars that reverberate to the strains of Coimbra's own distinctive version of *fado* (see page 131).

The principal courtyard of the university is marked by a bell tower and surrounded by historic buildings on three sides. At one end is the spectacular baroque **Biblioteca Joanina** (library; 9am–1pm and 2–5pm, last entry to the library 12.40pm and 4.40pm; http://visit.uc.pt), constructed in 1720 with João V's Brazilian wealth (also instrumental in building the great library at Mafra; see page 44). Three exquisitely gilded and painted chambers house some 300,000 leather-bound texts in many languages. On the same side of the courtyard are the **Museu de Arte Sacra** (Museum of Sacred Art) and the **Capela de São Miguel** (St Michael's Chapel), with fine *azulejos* and a massive baroque organ. Directly ahead is the highly ornate ceremonial hall, the **Sala Grande dos Actos** (same hours as the library), the heart of university life, where degrees are given out, and the **Sala do Exame Privado**, the Private Examination Room.

The nearby **Museu Nacional de Machado de Castro** (Tue–Sun Apr–Sept 10am–6pm, Oct–Mar 10am–12.30pm and

2–6pm; www.museumachadocastro.gov.pt/), housed in the former archbishop's palace, exhibits an excellent collection of medieval sculpture and religious paintings. Among the museum's complex of historic buildings are a Moorish tower and Roman crypt in a fascinating warren of underground passages.

On either side of the museum are Coimbra's two cathedrals, the classical-baroque **Sé Nova** (New Cathedral; Mon–Sat 10am–6.30pm, Sun 10am–12.30pm; free) and the vastly more interesting **Sé Velha** (Old Cathedral; Mon–Fri 10am–5.30pm, Sat until 6.30pm, Sun 11am–5pm; http://sevelha-coimbra.org). The fine Romanesque bulk of the old cathedral is reminiscent of the early Crusader-era cathedrals of Lisbon and Porto. Renaissance detail has been added around the portals, but the interior remains fairly stark. A chapel to the right contains a collection of impressive life-size stone carvings of Jesus, the Virgin Mary and the 12 disciples. Be sure not to miss the peaceful Romanesque cloister.

The single-nave **Igreja de Santa Cruz** (Mon–Sat 11.30am–4.30pm, Sun 2–5pm), built in 1131, is renowned for its dazzling Manueline detail, including an elaborate portico and carved pulpit. The church holds the tombs of Portugal's first and second kings, Afonso Henriques and Sancho I, and the Claustro de Silêncio (Cloister of Silence) is lined with pretty arches and colourful *azulejos*. Down towards the river, the **Jardim Botânico** (Botanical Garden; daily 9am–8pm, Oct–Mar to 5.30pm; free), with plants collected from across Portugal's far-flung empire, is Portugal's largest.

Across the river are the **Convento de Santa Clara-a-Velha** (Old Santa Clara convent; daily May–Sept 9am–7pm, Oct–Apr to 6pm), where the lifeless Inês de Castro was crowned (see page 47), and the newer, uphill **Convento de Santa Clara-a-Nova** (New Convent), where the silver tomb of Isabel, the sainted queen of Dom Dinis, can be found. Nearby is the **Quinta das Lágrimas**

estate, now an elegant hotel, where Inês was reputedly murdered. Legend holds that the garden's 'pool of tears', immortalised in the epic poem by Luís de Camões, is stained deep red by her blood. Also south of the river is **Portugal dos Pequeninos** (daily June–mid-Sept 9am–8pm, mid-Sept–Feb 10am–5pm, Mar–May 10am–7pm; www.portugaldospequenitos.pt), a children's theme park.

COIMBRA ENVIRONS

Portugal's largest and finest Roman ruins lie 17km (10 miles) south of Coimbra, at **Conimbriga** (daily 10am–7pm; free on Sun; www.conimbriga.gov.pt), close to the pottery town of Condeixa-a-Nova. Though the extensive site is still being excavated, remnants of fountains, thermal pools, a sophisticated heating system, a large villa and spectacular colourful mosaics – some of the finest under roofing at the Casa das Fontes – have been unearthed. Conimbriga had become a significant Roman town by 25BC, though many of the greatest finds here date to the 2nd and 3rd centuries AD. The museum boasts a superb collection of Roman artefacts including coins, pottery, weapons and glass.

Along the Mondego, 28km (17 miles) west of Coimbra, is the sturdy and imposing 14th-century castle at **Montemor-o-Velho** (daily 9.30am–6pm, winter until 5.30pm) with superb views.

One of Portugal's most ancient forests, land that inspires an almost mystical reverence for its citizens, is 25km (15 miles) north of Coimbra at **Buçaco** ➑. The dense, tranquil forest, criss-crossed with footpaths, has more than 700 types of trees and was once the preserve of Benedictine monks. Tucked in among the trees is the celebrated, fantastically ornate **Bussaco Palace Hotel** (see page 183), formerly a royal summer retreat, and a curious stone monastery, the Mosteiro dos Carmelitas. For further relaxation, the nearby town of **Luso** is full of elegant 19th-century buildings, a casino and thermal spas.

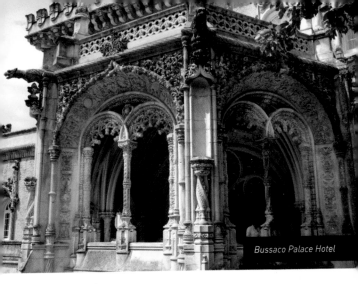
Bussaco Palace Hotel

THE COAST

The prettiest stretch of coast in the south of the Beira Litoral is near the ancient pine forest of the **Pinhal de Leiria**; superb beaches can be found at **São Pedro de Moel** (21km/13 miles north of Nazaré).

Figueira da Foz, 42km (26 miles) to the west of Coimbra at the mouth of the Mondego River, has developed from a fishing village into a lively resort popular with the Portuguese. The town beach is large, and separate smaller beaches cater to surfers and families.

Praia de Mira (35km/22 miles north of Figueira and 6km/4 miles west of the inland town of Mira) is situated by a small lagoon. Characterised by its wooden stilt-houses, it lacks the lively nightlife and accommodation of Figueira (camping is available), but makes up for it with unspoiled and uncrowded beaches and dunes.

Aveiro

A SALINEIRA

The main resort along this stretch of coast is historic **Aveiro**, 52km (32 miles) to the south of Porto and 29km (18 miles) north of Mira. Aveiro's unique way of life has developed around its large lagoon *(ria)*. The town was an important port until 1575, when a sandbar formed across the River Vouga, cutting the port off from the sea and creating a vast lagoon. A canal was cut in 1808, and the lagoon was traversed by Dutch-style canals and bridges.

The delightful **Municipal Museum** (Tue–Sun 10am–6pm), in the old Convento de Jesus, displays religious art, and includes the unusual 18th-century Chapel of Princesa Santa Joana. The tourist office on Rua João Mendonça can arrange boat trips to explore extensive salt pans and see the rich variety of birdlife. For a snack, which is popular with the locals, buy a small box of *ovos moles*, literally 'soft eggs' – sweet and irresistible.

BEIRA ALTA

On the way from Coimbra towards Viseu (87km/54 miles north-east), the land becomes emphatically rural. Small terraced farms, accompanied by stone houses, donkeys and grape vines, sit among forested hills. This is the Dão wine region, whose oaky red wines are named after the River Dão, a tributary of the Mondego.

Viseu ❾ is a dignified and historic town, supposedly home to Viriato, the Lusitanian hero who organised the opposition to the Roman invasion of 147BC. The scenic old town is centred around the **Praça da Sé**, with a central pillory and wealth of historic buildings. The bulky twin-towered cathedral (Mon–Sat 9am–1pm and 2–6pm, Sun 9.30am–noon and 2–7pm), originally Romanesque, was redesigned in the 17th century. The classical cloister has Ionic columns on the first level and Doric on the second. The other church on the square, the bright white **Igreja Misericórdia** (10am–12.30pm, 2–5.30pm), features a terrific baroque façade but an unprepossessing interior.

The top sight in Viseu, and one of Portugal's most important art museums, is the **Museu de Grão Vasco** (Tue 2–6pm, Wed–Sat 10am–1pm and 2–6pm, Sun 10am–2pm and 3–6pm), which

⊙ LAST OF THE MOLICEIROS

Not so long ago Aveiro's *ria*, or lagoon, was alive with fleets of flat, low, swan-necked sailing boats heaped with weed, to be used as fertiliser. The grace of these *moliceiros* was somewhat belied by wry jokes and cartoon figures painted on the prow, a local boatbuilders' tradition of considerable ancestry. With need for the lagoon's weed gone, the *moliceiros* soon went out of use. Yet, thanks to a few dedicated boatlovers and folk art fanciers, a few have survived. It's worth checking the lagoon shores or asking about them at the tourist office. Other lovely traditional boats still to be seen are the *meia lua* (half moon), a west coast surfboat used for fishing, and the Douro River's own *barco rabelo*, port-ferrying boats restored and maintained by port wine companies.

inhabits the former archbishop's palace next to the cathedral. Vasco Fernandes, more commonly referred to as Grão Vasco (the Great), founded the city's school of painting in the 16th century. Huge, bold panels of his work are on view, including 'São Pedro', 'Pentecost' and 'Assunção da Virgem', as are those of the various Flemish artists who influenced the Viseu School, and those of Vasco's great Portuguese rival, Gaspar Vaz. Perhaps the most interesting exhibit is the 14-panel depiction of the life of Christ, painted by the school of Grão Vasco in 1501–6 and transferred from the altar of the Viseu cathedral in the 18th century.

THE PLANALTO

Towards the northeast of the Beira Alta is the barren plateau of the **Planalto** ('High Plain'), a wild, cold and sparsely populated region, but important enough to have been fought over by Portugal and Spain. The plateau's isolation attracted many Jews fleeing the Inquisition.

The atmospheric walled town of **Trancoso** (43km/26 miles to the north of Guarda) records this heritage in the stone carvings above the doorways of Jewish houses. From miles around, you can see the powerful castle walls and strong keep, which was built by Dom Dinis to fortify the border against Spain.

Almeida (65km/40 miles east) also has well-preserved fortifications, a legacy of its position virtually on the Spanish border. The town is enclosed within star-shaped fortifications, reminiscent of those at Elvas in the Alentejo.

SERRA DA ESTRELA

The **Serra da Estrela**, just southwest of Guarda, incorporates Portugal's highest mountains, at 1,991m (6,532ft), and offers some fantastic scenery for hiking through the Parque Natural

(Natural Park). **Seia** makes a good base to explore the *serra*, as does **Penhas da Saúde**, the site of Portugal's only ski resort.

Linhares 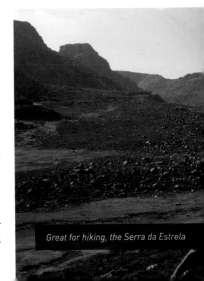, which dates from 1169, is one of Portugal's most appealing towns. Its moss-covered stone houses and tiny cobbled streets are preserved museum-like, though it still seems like a real town. Linhares has a stretch of Roman road and a scenic medieval castle with splendid views over granite peaks and the Rio Mondego valley. Details of hiking routes are available at the tourist office in Guarda or Covilhã, or at the park information offices in Gouveia, Manteigas or Seia.

Some 20km (12 miles) from Guarda is tiny **Belmonte**, with a carefully restored 13th-century castle and Jewish Quarter, still home to a Jewish community.

Covilhã, a further 20km (12 miles) south, has become a base for exploring the *serra* because of its location close to the highest peaks and the ski slopes. This mountainous area produced a couple of explorers who would help form the Portuguese empire: Pêro de Covilhã, who explored India and Ethiopia in the late 15th century, and Pedro Álvares Cabral who was born in Belmonte and discovered Brazil in 1500.

BEIRA BAIXA
Throughout the Lower Beira, wide agricultural

Great for hiking, the Serra da Estrela

plains and orchards stretch out between the rocky hills and sites of ancient settlements.

The main city in the region is **Castelo Branco**, invaded by the Spanish so often that little of historical interest survives. It is still a pleasant city, with small cobbled alleyways leading up to the ruined 'White Castle' at the highest point of the town. The **Paço Episcopal** (Bishop's Palace; Tue–Sun 10am–12.30pm and 2–5.30pm) is home to a regional museum, displaying a splendid collection of highly elaborate *colchas* (bedspreads), as well as 16th-century tapestries. The elegant formal Palace Gardens (9am–5pm, until 7pm in summer) are laid out with an array of baroque statues, sculpted hedges, fountains and pools. The nearby Miradouro de São Gens affords a good view of the city.

The atmospheric village of **Monsanto**, located about 50km (31 miles) to the northeast of Castelo Branco, balances on a dramatic rocky outcrop between massive boulders. The streets are too narrow for cars, but a short walk to the castle at the top is worth the effort for the impressive stonework and the view. A beautiful, but roofless, 13th-century Romanesque church can also be seen.

The granite boulders, some with tiny houses seemingly sealed between them, give Monsanto a unique atmosphere. Yet this village won a contest in 1938 to be named the nation's 'most Portuguese' village.

THE NORTH

PORTO

Portugal's prosperous second city, **Porto** ⑪ (also written Oporto in English, meaning 'the Port'), hugs the steep banks at the mouth of the Douro river. The former Roman settlement

of Portus, it combined with Calus, its twin town on the opposite bank, to become known as Portucale in the early Middle Ages.

With splendid bridges crossing the Douro and a red-roofed jumble of buildings creeping up the hillside, Porto contains a wonderful cocktail of architecture. Walking is the best way to explore it, despite the many hills that spill down to the river. The city has a new sense of vitality, with a spate of new architecture, art galleries and chic shops and restaurants, and a six-line Metro system that has been tunnelled through the city's granite.

The Douro that flows all the way from inland Spain has always been the source of Porto's wealth. The river snakes past the terraced vineyards of the Douro Valley, which produce fine table wines and, most famously, the rich fortified wine known as port. Traditionally port wine was shipped down river in oak barrels loaded on *barcos rabelos* (flat-bottomed square-sailed boats) to be stored in the cool and damp port lodges (merchants' warehouses) in Vila Nova de Gaia, across the river from Porto. The wine is still stored there, but transported by lorry.

The city, which began down by the river, has expanded considerably beyond the old walls. **Praça da Liberdade** (Liberty Square) in the upper level now marks the centre. Not far from here is the main tourist office, up Avenida dos Aliados and beside the City Hall, at Rua Clube dos Fenianos 25 (tel: 300 501 920, www.visitporto.travel). For a splendid view over the city's colourful jumble of streets and crumbling façades, head west out of the Praça, down Rua Clérigos, and climb the church bell tower of the baroque **Igreja de Clérigos** (daily 9am–7pm; www. torredosclerigos.pt/en/).

A couple of streets east of the tower (and south of the Praça da Liberdade) is the airy and ornate **Estação de São Bento**, far too handsome to be a mere railway hub. Completed in 1916, its

⊙ PORTO'S METRO

Much of this ancient city is best explored by walking – either in the city centre or even down to the Ribeiro, the colourful quarter on the Douro's northern bank. Yet the arrival of a Metro light rail transit system has not only cut down endless traffic jams – to Boavista, say – but has provided fast access to the airport and some of the city's greatest pleasures. One of these is the architecturally splendid concert hall, Casa da Mûsica. Another, attracting considerably larger crowds, is the world-famous Porto football stadium, Estádio do Dragão. You can also reach Vila Nova de Gaia on the Douro's south bank. The trains are clean and quiet. Purchasing tickets/electronic Andante cards is relatively straightforward (visit http://en.metrodoporto.pt). Note that they must be validated before you enter a train.

The azulejos inside Estação de São Bento

great entrance hall is decorated with wonderful *azulejo* panels depicting important scenes from the city's history.

Just south of the railway station is the Cathedral District. The 12th-century Romanesque **Sé** (Cathedral; Apr–Oct Mon–Sat 9am–7pm, Sun 9am–12.30pm and 2.30–7pm, winter Mon–Sat 9am–6pm, Sun 9am–12.30pm and 2.30–) is bare and austere – more fortress than church. In the 18th century, an attempt was made to improve its ponderous appearance with some baroque additions. Inside, a beautiful baroque silver altarpiece is worth a look, as is the rose window. Within these granite walls, João I married his English bride, Philippa of Lancaster, in 1387, thus sealing the ancient alliance between Portugal and England – an alliance with particular strength in Porto due to the overwhelming English involvement in the port wine trade.

Nearby, the **Casa-Museu Guerra Junqueiro** (Guerra Junqueiro Museum; Tue–Sun 10am–5.30pm) on Rua de Dom Hugo is the

18th-century home of the Portuguese poet, Guerra Junqueiro, where his furniture and art collection is on display. The church of **Santa Clara** (guided tours Mon–Fri 10am–12.30pm and 2.30–5pm, Sat 10am–12.30pm; free), on Largo 1 de Dezembro, remains a bit of a secret and a little difficult to find. Renaissance on the exterior, its exuberantly carved rococo interior is worth a look.

The riverside quay, the **Cais da Ribeira**, is an intriguing and atmospheric area popular with tourists and diners. The old quays, a Unesco World Heritage Site, have a number of seafood restaurants. Tour boats tie up here and offer short river tours, beneath the city's scenic bridges, as well as week-long trips up the Douro to Régua (see page 168). The impressive **Ponte Dom Luís I** (a 172m/564ft bridge built in 1886) looms over the colourful houses of the Ribeira to the river's south bank and the port

Barcos rabelos moored on the Douro

lodges *(caves)* of Vila Nova de Gaia are located.

Just uphill from the river is the **Bolsa** district, named after the elegant 19th-century **Palácio da Bolsa** (Stock Exchange; daily summer 9am–6.30pm, winter 9am–12.30pm and 2–5.30pm; www.palaciodabolsa.pt) on the Praça do Infante Dom Henrique. The ornate neo-classical building no longer functions as a stock exchange, but guided tours show visitors around the opulent interior. The highlight is the **Salão Árabe** (Arab Room) set in the lavish Moorish style of the Alhambra in Granada.

Ponte Dom Luís I

Next door is the city's finest church, the **Igreja de São Francisco** (daily Mar–May and Oct 9am–7pm, June 9am–7.30pm, July–Sep 9am–8pm, Nov–Feb 9am–6pm), on Rua do Infante D. Henrique. Conventionally Gothic on the outside, the church's interior is like an explosion in a gold factory. Gilded rococo details swathe the walls from floor to ceiling. The most impressive feature is the 'Tree of Jesse', an elaborately carved, gilded and painted 18th-century wood sculpture on the northern wall. This eye-catching piece depicts the family genealogy of Christ. Opposite the church is an interesting, small museum which holds relics of the old monastery and catacombs.

Also near the Bolsa is the **Casa do Infante** (Tue–Sun 9.30am–1pm and 2–5.30pm, Sun 2–5pm; free weekends), supposedly the site where Henry the Navigator was born. Citizens of Porto are very proud of their association with Henry, especially since their city was where the fleet for the 1415 assault on Ceuta was fitted out. For this patriotic venture against the Moors of North Africa, the people of Porto surrendered the finest cuts of meat in their stores to the navy and lived on tripe instead, thus earning the nickname of *tripeiros* (literally 'tripe eaters').

Some of Porto's other interesting museums are northwest of the centre. The **Museu Soares dos Reis** (on Rua Dom Manuel II; Tue–Sun 10am–6pm; free www.museusoaresdosreis.gov.pt) has a wonderful collection of fine art housed in an 18th-century Palácio dos Carrancas. Portuguese artists from the 15th to the 20th century are well represented, including paintings by Josefa de Óbidos and sculptures by António Soares dos Reis. Look for his *O Desterrado*, a thoughtful work in marble.

The **Museu Romântico da Quinta da Macieirinha**, Rua Entre-Quintas 220 (west of Clérigos; Mon–Sat 10am–5.30pm, Sun 10am–12.30pm and 2–5.30pm; free weekends), displays a collection of 19th-century art and furniture in the last home of the deposed King of Sardinia.

Casa de Música

Casa de Música (www.casadamusica.com), a gleaming-white 1,300-seat auditorium with perfect acoustics designed by Rem Koolhaas, hosts the best international orchestras. For many it is an architectural marvel but some liken it to a meteorite crashed into the middle of the city.

Further removed but well worth seeking out for lovers of modern art and architecture, the **Fundação Serralves** (Rua D. João de Castro, 210, about 3km/2 miles west of Torre de Clérigos; Tue–Fri 10am–6pm, Sat-Sun 10am–7pm; free first Sun of the month 10am–1pm; www.serralves.pt) has two primary parts. One is a stark modern shell built by the famed local architect Álvaro Siza Vieira and the other a fabulous pink 1930s art deco building, surrounded by lovely gardens and a park populated with goats. Both exhibition spaces house temporary shows by Portuguese and international contemporary artists.

A great place to sample port is at the **Port & Douro Wines Institute** (Mon–Fri 11am–7pm; www.ivdp.pt) at Rua Ferreira Borges. Also fantastic is **Graham's Lodge** (Vila Nova de Gaia; by reservation only – visit www.grahams-port.com), located on the hill near the Douro riverbank, which offers fabulous views over the city and the iconic Dom Luís I bridge linking Porto with Gaia.

A quiet backstreet, Porto

VILA NOVA DE GAIA

The lower level of the Dom Luís I Bridge leads to the wine cellars of **Vila Nova de Gaia**, the low buildings on the southern bank. Familiar and less familiar names – Taylor, Osborne and Ramos Pinto – appear on the roofs. The modern riverside restaurants have a good view across to the city. Beaches along the Atlantic coast of Vila Nova de Gaia are clean; many have obtained the blue flag.

Although it is no longer required by law, most port is still blended, stored and aged in the **port wine lodges** of Gaia (as the riverfront town is commonly called). Almost all were founded after the Treaty of Methuen in 1703, under which the English agreed to reduce the tariffs on port wine imports. Most winemakers offer free tours of their lodges and offer visitors a free sample.

⊘ THE SECRETS OF PORT WINE

The Douro Valley, which produces the grapes that make port wine, became the world's first demarcated wine-growing region in 1757. Port is now legendary among wines, and a good reason to visit the Douro Valley is to taste or indulge in a variety of ports – such as vintage ports, aged tawnys and late bottle vintages –and to learn about the winemaking traditions. A 'Port Wine Route' (Rota do Vinho do Porto) links a number of atmospheric *quintas* (vineyard estates) in the valley; some offer accommodation (see page 180).

The valley's freezing winters and blisteringly hot summers create a unique microclimate that produces intensely flavourful grapes. The inability to recreate these conditions elsewhere is why true port wine only comes from the north of Portugal. In late September and early October, whole communities gather for the harvest *(vindima)*. Though most grapes are now mechanically crushed, some small vintners still crush them by foot in giant pressing tanks, in a jubilant atmosphere accompanied by singing and guitar music (and of course, drinking).

Port is a fortified wine; winemakers long ago added grape brandy to stabilise the wines during their long journeys overseas and discovered that the brandy halted fermentation and produced a fresh sweet flavour that deepened with age. For more information, visit www.ivdp.pt.

COASTAL EXCURSIONS

Porto's nearest beaches lie to the west, where the Douro passes a large sandbar and meets the sea at **Foz do Douro** (Mouth of the Douro). In the 19th century, Foz was a very popular resort, but the water is heavily polluted. Nevertheless, the beaches and restaurants still make an enjoyable day or evening out. Public buses (1M, 200, 202) link the resort to

Barrels in a port-wine lodge

the 17th-century **Castelo do Queijo** (Cheese Castle).

Further north, the beach resorts of the Minho's Costa Verde are at least clean, even if none too warm. The nearest one to Porto is the twin resort area of Vila do Conde/Póvoa de Varzim, 27km (16 miles) to the north. **Vila do Conde** is the decidedly more pleasant and less developed of the two.

Póvoa do Varzim, a short walk north from Vila do Conde, is a much livelier and more built-up resort with a casino. An interesting diversion inland from here is to **Rates**, where there is a beautiful 11th-century Romanesque church.

THE DOURO VALLEY

The **Douro Valley**, extending along the river east toward the Spanish border, is one of the most attractive regions in Portugal. Sprinkled with small villages, impressive *quintas* (agricultural estates) and lined with beautifully terraced

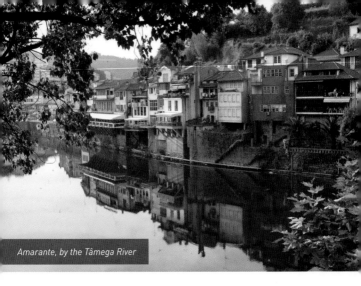

Amarante, by the Tâmega River

vineyards, the valley is a Unesco World Heritage Site. Cruises run from the Ribeira waterfront in Porto, up to Régua and Pinhão, or between Pinhão all the way to Pocinho, near the Spanish border. A spectacular train ride travels the length of the valley. Contact the tourist office in Porto for details.

Upriver from the sandbank at its mouth, the Douro runs between Porto and the port lodges of Vila Nova de Gaia, passing beneath a series of impressive bridges and on towards port wine territory. The railway line from Porto skips the first 60km (37 miles) of the river – but this is the least interesting stretch. The line eventually joins the river near **Ribadouro**, proceeding along the northern bank, past small towns and fields where the haystacks, set on cross-shaped supports, look from a distance like scarecrows.

Attractive **Amarante** sits on a gorge of the Tâmega (a tributary of the Douro) and makes a good stop if you are driving along the road from Porto towards Mesão Frio and Régua. Baronial mansions with gaily painted balconies overlooking the river line the streets. Rising above a handsome stone arched bridge and leafy park, the former 16th-century monastery of **São Gonçalo** has been renovated and now houses an interesting Museum of Contemporary Art (Museo Amadeo de Souza-Cardoso; 9.30am–12.30pm and 2–5.30pm, until 6pm in summer; www.amadeosouza-cardoso.pt).

The river bends and twists, widens and narrows among green terraced hills. The port trade prompted the growth of **Peso da Régua** (usually called just Régua), 70km (43 miles) east of Porto. Régua was once the main port used to ship young wines down river in *barcos rabelos* (flat-bottomed wooden boats) to Vila Nova de Gaia. The railway then took over from Pinhão (at the confluence of the Douro and Pinhão rivers), and now the wine goes mostly by road.

Industrial Régua has long been a port production hub, though the centre for quality port has now shifted to Pinhão. The headquarters of port winemakers, Casa do Douro, are here, and Sandeman operates a modern winery across the river. From March to November, many river cruises stop off here; check with the Porto tourist office.

Mesão Frio, 12km (7 miles) west of Régua, is the gateway to the Douro. Sitting high above the river, amid the rambling hills of the Serra do Marão, it has a number of beautiful *solares* (manor houses), some of which offer accommodation.

The prettiest town in the area is the affluent centre of **Lamego** ⑫, south of the Douro, 13km (8 miles) from Régua. Although technically part of the Beiras region, Lamego's soul belongs to the Douro. As well as growing grapes for port, Lamego also produces a fine sparkling wine called Raposeira. The town was once a pilgrimage centre, a heritage reflected in one of Portugal's most famous churches, the baroque **Nossa Senhora dos Remédios** and the stunning stone staircase that climbs the hill. Inspired by another shrine, Bom Jesus (see page 83) near Braga, the monumental staircase is lined with statues, *azulejos*, fountains and chapels. Some penitents still heroically climb the 600-plus steps on their knees, especially during the great annual pilgrimage on 8 September.

Lamego has a wealth of handsome baroque mansions, as well as a scenic 13th-century castle and a 16th-century cathedral) with a 12th-century tower. The **Museu de Lamego** (daily 10am–6pm; www.museudelamego.pt) in the old bishop's palace houses a fine collection of Flemish tapestries and religious statues, as well as paintings by Grão Vasco of the Viseu school.

Pinhão, upriver from Régua (both the train trip and drive along this stretch of river are stunning), is an enjoyable little town with deep connections to the port wine trade. The tiny railway station displays *azulejos* depicting the harvest, and many important *quintas* owned by the biggest port concerns, as well as independently owned vineyards, hug the hills. Vintage House, a 19th-century mansion, contains an excellent hotel and restaurant.

From Pinhão to Pocinho, the train snakes along the Douro's switchbacks with magnificent views at every turn (two hours return trip). Another good route is north to Tua.

Having little to do with wine, but plenty to do with the historic underpinnings of this region, is the **Parque Arqueológico do Vale do Côa** ⑬ (archaeological park; www.arte-coa.pt), with its sublime Paleolithic rock drawings, near **Vila Nova de Foz Côa** (8km/5 miles south of Pocinho). Discovered only in 1992, the engravings of deer, goats and horses constitute the largest outdoor assembly of Paleolithic rock art in Europe.

Visits are by guided tour only, through the headquarters of the foundation overseeing the project. Attendance is strictly

Ponte de Lima and its namesake Roman bridge

limited, and slots to visit the three sites are often reserved weeks in advance. To arrange a visit stop by the park's headquarters in Vila Nova de Foz Côa (Avenida Gago Coutinho e Sacadura Cabral, 19A; tel: 279 768 260/1; email: visitas. pavc@arte-coa.pt). Visits last an hour and a half (to each site, arranged separately) and transport to the sites is included. A combined ticket also allows entry to the museum (Tue–Sun 9am–5.30pm) which has cutting-edge displays on the rock paintings, temporary exhibitions, and an excellent restaurant.

THE MINHO

The lush northwestern province of the Minho north of Porto is one of the most beautiful regions of Portugal. The intensely green area is renowned for its mountains and forests, *vinho verde* ('green wine') and Costa Verde ('Green Coast').

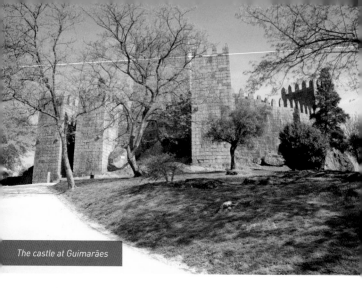

The castle at Guimarães

Portugal originated in this corner just below Galicia, the one-time Celtic settlement in Spain. It was recaptured from the Moors early in the Christian Reconquest campaign and, when Afonso Henriques declared himself the first king in 1139, the Minho became the independent state of Portucale (covering an area from the Douro to the River Minho). The region is said to be one of the most religious and conservative in Portugal.

GUIMARÃES

A large sign in the centre of **Guimarães** (49km/30 miles north-east of Porto) declares 'Aqui Nasceu Portugal' ('Here was born Portugal'), testament to the historic nature of this medieval gem of a small city.

The city's compact yet sturdy 10th-century **castle** (daily 10am–6pm; free first Sun of the month) seems to have grown out of the rocky hillock. Seven towers protect a large central keep lined with unusual triangular battlements that resemble serrated teeth. Afonso Henriques, the first king of Portugal, is said to have been born in the castle and baptised nearby, in the small Romanesque **Igreja de São Miguel do Castelo** (daily 9.30am–5.30pm).

Just down the hill is the massive **Paço dos Duques de Bragança** (Ducal Palace; daily 10am–6pm; free on first Sunday of the month), a mix between a French château and a crusader castle. Once the home of the Dukes of Bragança, it fell into disrepair and was reconstructed from ruin in the 1930s as a palace for Salazar. It now houses a large collection of antiques.

The historic city centre extends down the hill from the castle along the Rua de Santa Maria to a series of beautiful medieval squares surrounded by old townhouses. The triangular **Largo de Santiago** is flanked by the arcaded 14th-century old town hall and a series of townhouses converted into an inn called the Pousada da Oliveira.

Through the arcades is the central **Largo da Oliveira**, where the excellent **Museu Alberto Sampaio** (Tue–Sun 10am–6pm; free on Sun 10am–2pm) is located in Nossa Senhora da Oliveira (the Collegiate Church of Our Lady of the Olive Tree). The museum houses stone carvings from the convent in a 13th-century cloister, as well as gold, ceramics and religious items. There is also a room devoted to the battle of Aljubarrota (see page 48); exhibits include the shirt said to have been worn by João I during the fray.

Green wine

Vinho verde, the Minho's sparkling 'green wine', made from grapes mainly grown on wire vine supports, as well as pretty bowers, has many attributes. Refreshing, only lightly alcoholic, it also has a red version, *vinho tinto*, best enjoyed with a hearty meal.

The other notable museum in Guimarães is the **Museu Martins Sarmento** (Tue–Sat 9.30am–noon and 2–5pm; Sun 10am–120pm and 2–5pm), named after the 19th-century excavator of the Citânia de Briteiros, an ancient settlement of Celto-Iberians. Artefacts displayed include carved stone lintels, tools and several fascinating sculptures, such as the enormous pre-Roman Colossus of Pedralva. A nearby Plataforma das Artes e Criatividade located in a splendidly converted old market is a multifunctional centre hosting art exhibitions, cultural and social events, as well as Coleção José de Guimarães (www.ciajg.pt; Tue–Sun 10am–1pm and 2–7pm), an interesting collection of African, Precolombian and ancient Chinese art.

In the Penha Hills above the city is the lovely **Mosteiro de Santa Marinha da Costa**, founded in the 12th century. This lovely former monastery has been remarkably restored to form one of Portugal's most evocative *pousadas*. The views of Guimarães down the hill are outstanding. The most enjoyable way up to Penha, which is 5km (3 miles) by road, is to take the fast *teleférico* (cable

Artsy diversion

About 14 km (8.7 miles) south west of Guimarães in the small town of Santo Tirso, world famous architects Álvaro Siza Vieira and Eduardo Souto de Moura converted an historic Portuguese monastery into the Museu Municipal Abade Pedrosa (MMAP; Tue–Fri 9am–5.30pm, Sat–Sun 2–7pm; www.cm-stirso.pt). The museum has an interesting archaeological collection which includes prehistoric sculptures, ceramics and coins found in the region. The complex also contains the International Museum of Contemporary Sculpture (MIEC; same hours as MMAP; http://miec.cm-stirso.pt) which contains works by Portuguese and international artists.

car; www.turipenha.pt).
Catch it at the end of Rua de
Doutor José Sampaio.

BRITEIROS

Just 15km (9 miles) from
Guimarães on the way to
Braga is the prehistoric
site of **Briteiros** (Oct–Mar
9am–5pm, Apr–Sep 9am–
6pm), set on a rocky hillside overlooking a series of
valleys and forested hills.
Inhabited by Celt-Iberians
from around the 4th cen-
tury BC to the 4th century

The delightful old town of Braga

AD, the entire hillside is covered with the remains of the best-
preserved *citânia* (Celtic hill settlement) in Portugal. The walls of
more than a hundred circular houses are visible – two have been
rebuilt to give an idea of what the settlement once looked like – in
addition to roads, drainage channels and a defensive wall.

BRAGA

Gracious and bustling **Braga ⑭** (22km/13 miles northwest
of Guimarães) is the 12th-century ecclesiastical centre of
Portugal, today famous for its Holy Week celebrations. It has
more than 30 churches to bolster its religious reputation. The
old town, which is peppered with several fine turn-of-the-cen-
tury cafés on or near Praça República (including Café Astoria
and A Brasileira), is a delight to wander around.

The original Romanesque exterior of the cathedral (daily
9.30am–12.30pm and 2.30–5.30pm, until 6.30pm in summer;

Bom Jesus do Monte

www.se-braga.pt) has been embellished over the years in a number of styles. Inside are two extravagant golden organs, replete with trumpets, a carved choir of Brazil wood and a painted ceiling flanking the nave near the entrance.

The true wealth of the Archbishopric of Braga, though, can be glimpsed in the cathedral's stunning **Tesouro da Catedral** (Cathedral Treasury; same hours as the cathedral), crammed with gold and silver pieces, including the cross that Cabral took on his pioneering voyage to Brazil in 1500, polychromatic figures and *azulejos*. Across a courtyard are a couple of 14th-century chapels, one with a tomb of the parents of the first King of Portugal and the other a mummified archbishop who died in 1397.

The pedestrian-only Rua do Souto runs right through the middle of town, passing the square of the former **Archbishop's Palace**, nowadays a public library, and an old medieval keep. Before reaching the centre at the Praça da República, you will find the tourist office housed in a marvellous art deco building.

Braga is known for its churches, but it has many splendid Baroque mansions as well. Just west of city centre is **Palácio dos Biscainhos**, built in the 17th century (the decoration is 18th-century). The house reflects the refined lifestyle enjoyed by the nobility, and now houses the interesting municipal museum

(Tue–Sun 9.30am–12.45pm and 2–5.30pm). South of Praça da República is the magnificently blue-tiled **Casa do Raio**. The town also has the fascinating Diogo de Sousa Archaeological Museum (Rua dos Bombeiros Voluntários; daily 9.30am–5.30pm) housing ancient artefacts found locally, including Roman milestones. A short walk from here are the **Termas Romanas** (http://bragaro mana.cm-braga.pt; Tue–Fri 9am–1pm, 2–6pm, Sat–Sun 10am–5pm), dating from the 2nd century AD.

Beyond Braga is one of the north's most iconic sights, the 18th-century pilgrimage church of **Bom Jesus do Monte**, (winter 9am–6pm, summer 8am–7pm; free), situated in the mountains 4km (2 miles) east of Braga. The twin-towered baroque church is principally notable for the grand staircase that leads up to it. It is lined with chapels that feature the 14 Stations of the Cross, lichen-covered statues, urns and fountains. The devout sometimes climb all the way up to the church on their knees; the less committed (and less able) can walk or take the funicular railway and stay in one of the three hotels, which are located at the top.

BARCELOS

West of Braga toward the coast is **Barcelos**, home of the country's largest agricultural market (held every Thursday in the massive open square, the Campo da República). Every kind of animal and piles of produce from the Minho is on sale, as well as the famous pottery and handicrafts of Barcelos. The town is the source of Portugal's ubiquitous black-and-red cockerels.

In one corner of the square is the beautiful church of **Nossa Senhor Bom Jesus da Cruz**, an octagonal baroque building. The old part of town continues on down to the River Cávado. The Palace of the Counts of Barcelos overlooks the river, but was abandoned after the 1755 earthquake. Its shell now houses the various stone artefacts making up the open-air **Museu Arqueológico** (daily, free).

Folk dancers in Viana do Castelo

Not to be missed is the pottery museum, the **Museu de Olaria** (www.museuolaria. pt; Tue–Fri 10am–5.30pm, Sat–Sun 10am–12.30pm and 2–5.30pm), featuring traditional ceramics and pottery from all over the country.

THE MINHO COAST

The Minho's **Costa Verde** (Green Coast) is low-key compared with the crowded beaches of the Algarve. Beautiful beaches run in a virtually unbroken sweep from Porto all the way up to the Galician (Spanish) border on the River Minho.

The only major resort along this coastline is the splendid city of **Viana do Castelo** ⓑ (60km/38 miles north of Porto). Viana is bounded by the estuary of the River Lima to the south and by the wooded Monte de Santa Luzia to the north. The triangular Praça da República forms the centre of the historic old town, surrounded by *palácios* constructed during Viana's heyday in the 15th century as a *bacalhau* fishing centre. Especially interesting are the fine 16th-century Renaissance Misericórdia (Almshouse) and Gothic Igreja Matriz.

Rising above Viana is the scenic **Monte de Santa Luzia**. Like Bom Jesus, it has a pilgrimage church on the summit and a funicular railway, but no grand staircase. Though the church itself isn't remarkable, the views from the plaza in front are all encompassing. There is also a fine hotel (see page 185) and an excavated *citânia* (pre-Roman hillfort) faintly reminiscent of Briteiros.

Viana's main beach lies to the south, across the estuary at **Praia do Cabedelo**, accessible by ferry or road. North along the coast from Viana there is little sand, but the rocks are popular for fishing. The small quaint resort town of **Vila Praia de Âncora** is 16km (10 miles) further up the coast.

THE RIVER LIMA

Inland from Viana, the beautiful flat Lima Valley runs east through a gentle agricultural landscape. The Romans settled this attractive area and built a bridge at **Ponte de Lima**, 23km (14 miles) upstream from Viana. A Roman bridge *(ponte)* still spans the Lima, though the town is perhaps better known for its ancient bi-monthly market. The hills on the north side offer

⊙ THE FINEST OF FOLK FAIRS

Agreeably located at the mouth of the river Limae, Viana do Castelo's annual folk fair (held each August) provides the town's most shining moments, honouring patron saint *Nossa Senhora da Agonia*. Processions and parades take place over several days, the highlight of each being the striking costumes worn by the women, some escorted by their dashing menfolk. Often, the costumes display vivid embroidery – an informed eye will know from where the young women come. Children take part, too, in their own bright folk costumes. Farm carts and fishing folk are also represented. Strangest and most impressive of all are the so-called brides in black – smiling women, clad in black gowns and wearing a wealth of gold jewellery on their arms and around their necks.

scenic walks, and Ponte de Lima has an excellent choice of accommodation in old manor houses.

Ponte da Barca (18km/11 miles further east along the Lima) is also an appealing town. It has a fine 15th-century bridge and also hosts a bi-monthly market by the river. The town serves as a good base for some pleasant hill walks, past small, unspoiled Minho villages.

THE PENEDA-GERÊS NATIONAL PARK

The Lima Valley continues east towards the river's source in Spain, passing through the wild and wonderful **Peneda-Gerês National Park**. The park is one of the most visited parts of the Minho, yet it is very easy to hike up into the mountains and find yourself alone with the mountain goats. The park has moun-

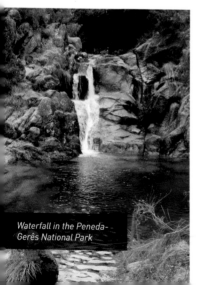

tains, river valleys, mega-lithic monuments (antas), waterfalls and small mountain hamlets. Fifteen species of wild flowers are unique to the park, which is crisscrossed by numerous tracks that pass reservoirs perfect for a dip after a long day's hike.

The park is divided into two parts: the much-visited **Serra do Gerês** and the quieter, wilder **Serra da Peneda** to the north. **Caldas do Gerês** is the principal tourist base, a slightly tattered spa town.

Waterfall in the Peneda-Gerês National Park

Hiking advice is available from the park information office, and the tourist office can provide details of accommodation and outdoor activities, such as horse trekking and kayaking. The nearby **Miradouro do Gerês** has a splendid view over much of the park.

The best approach to the northern Peneda section of the park is from either Monção or Melgaço, on the River Minho. The main point of access for the eastern part of the park is Caldas do Gerês, but another fascinating route starts from the Roman spa town of Chaves, close to the Spanish border in Trás-os-Montes, and crosses a truly remote area passing by the gigantic **Pisões dam**.

> ### Peneda-Gerês National Park
>
> For adventure activities in the **Peneda-Gerês National Park**, try Equi Campo (tel: 253 161 405; www.equi campo.com) and campsite Parque Campismo de Cerdeira (tel: 253 351 005; www.parquecerdeira.com), both in **Campo do Gerês**.

THE RIVER MINHO

The River Minho forms the northern border between the Minho (Portugal) and Galicia (Spain). Its banks are lined with numerous beautiful walled towns and imposing fortresses, once a powerful deterrent against invaders. The charming town of **Vila Nova de Cerveira**, situated approximately 20km (12 miles) northeast from the coastal resort of Vila Praia de Âncora, is typical of them, with thick town walls and a regular ferry service across the river to Spain. Impressively located inside the walls of the old fortress is a luxurious *pousada*.

Further upriver, **Valença do Minho** has dramatic and powerful defensive walls (also housing a *pousada*). Within is a well-preserved town of winding streets and quaint 17th-century buildings.

TRÁS-OS-MONTES

The name given to Trás-os-Montes – 'Beyond the Mountains' – suggests how remote, and even forgotten, it is, even in this small country. Portugal's poorest region is one of deep river valleys separated by rocky hilltops and dense forests. Despite modernisation of recent years, the region retains a sleepy medieval air and a traditional agricultural way of life.

The land is divided by temperature: the northern part, Terra Fria ('Cold Land'), experiences very harsh winters, while Terra Quente ('Hot Land') is more temperate, containing large vineyards in the Upper Douro Valley. The white almond blossom in

◎ SAINTS DAYS, FAIRS AND FESTAS

Every city, town and village in Portugal has its own saint's day and it is always celebrated with food, copious wine, loud music and general jollity. Fireworks, too, usually. In Lisbon, especially in Alfama, native son Sant'António in mid-June prompts the partying and parades, the *Marchas Populares*. In Porto, 24 June is loud for São João, St John. Each town and village erupts when its day comes: local traditions call for colour – horsy gatherings in the Ribatejo towns south of the Tagus, the dancing of *pauliteiros*, tough men in petticoats and shawls in Miranda do Douro – whose religious procession includes a tiny top-hatted Jesus, *Menino Jesus da Cartolinha*, normally kept with a fine wardrobe of clothes in the church. In northern Trás-os-Montes, boys dress up in masks and rags to tease the local girls. In the south, more than one village *festa* is scented with the aroma of barbecued *chouriço* (sausage) and the strong, distinctive odour of grilled sardines.

spring is one of the most sublime sights in Portugal.

VILA REAL AND THE SOUTHWEST

Vila Real ⑯ is the largest town in the region. Mostly modern and industrial, it sits on the edge of the impressive deep gorge of the River Corgo, which is a tributary of the Douro. The town is surrounded by several interesting sights, and the Alvão and Marão mountain ranges rise up

Praça de Camões, Chaves

just outside, making it an excellent base for hiking and climbing.

At the centre of the town is the broad Avenida Carvalho Araújo, where you will find the cathedral and tourist office in an old mansion. If you continue south, you will pass the 14th-century **Capela de São Bras** and be rewarded with a fine view of the gorge.

The top sight in the area is the magnificent 18th-century baroque manor house known as the **Casa de Mateus** (daily Apr–Oct 9am–7pm, rest of the year until 5pm; www.casade mateus.com), just 3km (2 miles) from Vila Real. The early 18th-century Italianate façade will be familiar to many: it appears on bottles of Mateus Rosé wine (although there is no connection), which has long been among Portugal's leading exports. You can take a tour of the interior, which has several notable salons and a well-stocked library, but the exterior and formal gardens set in a vast farm are the outstanding features. Built by the counts of Vila Real, the palace is owned by the Mateus

Foundation, which organises a number of cultural activities. Wine and Port tastings are available.

CHAVES AND ENVIRONS

Beyond Vila Real, Trás-os-Montes becomes noticeably wilder. The main road to Chaves follows a scenic route along the valley of the Corgo. **Vidago** is an elegant 19th-century spa town, 17km (11 miles) before Chaves, with the renovated, grandiose Edwardian Palace Hotel, gardens, spa and an eighteen-hole golf course.

Chaves, 12km (7 miles) from Spain, is a quiet place – at least it is now that it isn't suffering repeated attacks from the invading Spanish. The last military attack took place in 1912, but waves of Spanish shoppers still invade the town every weekend in search of bargain prices on a number of goods. The town's strategic role as a border crossing is reflected in its name (*chaves* means 'keys') and by its two 17th-century fortresses. There is also a 14th-century keep, which today houses an interesting **Military Museum**.

Chaves was an important Roman spa town, known as Aquae Flaviae; its hot springs are good for rheumatism and gout. The Romans also built a bridge over the River Tâmega, which is still in use and retains its ancient milestone. You can learn more about the town's Roman past in the **Museu da Região Flaviense** (Regional Museum; Mon–Fri 9am–12.30pm and 2–5.30pm; Sat–Sun 2–5.30pm) on Praça Camões. The attractive, well-maintained old town

Very superstitious

Remote Portugal remains profoundly superstitious. Even with countrywide television old ways sometimes die hard. You can still come across *curandeiras*, healers with a wide knowledge of herbs, and *bruxas* (witches) were familiar figures well into the 20th century.

also has several interesting medieval squares and two fine churches.

Long before the Romans arrived, the region's pre-historic inhabitants left a series of carvings on a massive granite boulder at **Outeiro Machado**, 3km (2 miles) outside Chaves. The carved symbols are believed to have been associated with rituals involving sacrifice – easy to believe in this otherworldly setting.

Wheat fields near Bragança

BRAGANÇA AND THE NORTHEAST

The route from Chaves to Bragança is particularly attractive: the road winds over mountain passes, through pine forests and past the spines of bare, rocky hillsides.

Bragança ⓱ is a remote outpost, but one with a grand history. It was here that Catherine of Bragança, the wife of the English king, Charles II, was born. She took with her to England the custom of drinking afternoon tea, and her dowry included Bombay, thus beginning England's interest in India. Catherine's family served as rulers of Portugal between 1640 and 1910, but they preferred their estate at Vila Viçosa in the Alentejo to this lonely vastness.

The town is dominated by its **Citadel** (Cidadela), one of the best-known in Portugal, and by the bleak surrounding hills. The fortress encloses a small, medieval village of whitewashed houses where tourists still raise eyebrows. The central keep

Bragança's Citadel

sits on the highest ground and houses an interesting **Museu Militar** (Tue–Sun 9am–noon and 2–5pm), tracing the course of Portuguese military concerns from prehistoric times right through to the colonial wars of the 1970s. In front of the keep is Portugal's most curious pillory *(pelourinho)*, which stands on top of a primitive granite boar *(javali)*, carved in prehistoric times.

Also within the castle is **Igreja de Santa Maria**, which has wavy entrance columns and a lovely painted ceiling. Next door stands a rare example of a 12th-century **meeting house** *(domus municipalis)*, the only surviving Romanesque civic building in Portugal. It has five sides, and the upper floor, decorated with Romanesque arches under a timber roof, was used for assemblies, while the lower floor served as a water cistern.

In the lower town, the unusual **Museu Regional Abade de Baçal** (Tue–Fri 9.30am–5.30pm, Sat–Sun 9.30am–6pm;) is located in the former Bishop's Palace. The abbot was quite a collector; on display is an eclectic mix of local archaeological finds, clerical items, regional paintings and costumes.

Two churches to visit are the Renaissance **Igreja de São Bento**, with a contrasting ceiling, part Moorish carved wood and part trompe l'oeil; and the **Igreja de São Vicente**, where Pedro I claimed to have married Inês de Castro (see page 47). The **Centro Ciência Viva** (www.braganca.cienciaviva.pt) celebrates the city's economic reliance on silk from the 15th to the 19th centuries, while the **Centro de Arte Contemporânea Graça Morais** (Tue–Sun 10am–6.30pm; http://centroartegraca morais.cm-braganca.pt) has a permanent exhibition of paintings by the local artist Graça Morais.

The barren and wild **Parque Natural de Montesinho** lies between Bragança and Spain, and is home to a number of small, isolated villages that have strived to keep up their long-held traditions of communal ownership and pre-Christian ritual. The villagers share this fascinating landscape with wolves and wild boars. For hardcore hikers, the trails of Montesinho are a delight. For details of campsites, visit the park office in Bragança.

Tiny **Rio de Onor**, 24km (15 miles) to the northeast, is a village that time has forgotten and, at the same time, is a geographical oddity. The town straddles the border: half is in Portugal, half in Spain (where it's called Rihonor de Castilla). Locals have long gone back and forth between Portuguese and Spanish, with intermarriage between the two nationalities common.

MIRANDA DO DOURO

About as far east as you can get in Trás-os-Montes, **Miranda do Douro** stands poised at the edge of the great gorge of the Alto Douro (Upper Douro). Halfway across the modern dam, Spain begins.

The gorge at Miranda do Douro

Miranda itself is officially a 'city', even though it only has around 7,000 inhabitants. Their low whitewashed houses and cobbled streets were once enclosed by walls to keep the Spanish out – a purpose that failed in 1762, when a force of French and Spanish troops blew up the castle, leaving it a fairly uninspiring ruin. The event led Miranda to lose its bishop, who decamped to the safety of Bragança. The cold, dark and austere 16th-century **Sé** (cathedral) remains. In the right-hand transept, in a glass case, is a curiosity, a small statue of a boy known as the Menino Jesus da Cartolina. Sporting hand-tailored clothes of a tiny dandy, the little figure commemorates a 16th-century boy-hero who is said to have saved the city from the Spanish. Locals believed he was Jesus in disguise.

On Largo Dom João III, at the centre of the town, is the excellent **Museu da Terra de Miranda** (Tue 2–6pm, Wed–Sun 9am–1pm and 2–6pm; www.culturanorte.pt), displaying a selection of traditional Mirandês costumes, ancient ritualistic figures, furniture and folklore objects.

Miranda has its own culture and a distinctive dialect, Mirandês, that freely combines Latin, Portuguese, Spanish and even some Hebrew. The town is also renowned for its festivals and unique stick dancers, called the *pauliteiros*.

The **gorge** itself is about 2km (1 mile) away, down a twisting road. The rocky hillsides on both sides of the dam are home to some 80 species of birds, as well as flocks of sheep. You can take river boat cruises along the gorge – ask at the tourist office for details. On the other side of the dam, the river snakes its way through port-wine country down to Porto.

CENTRAL AND SOUTHEASTERN TRÁS-OS-MONTES

Mirandela is a pleasant town at the hub of the region's road system, 54km (33 miles) southeast of Chaves, 64km (40 miles) southwest of Bragança and 70km (43 miles) northeast of Vila Real. The town lies among orchards in the valley of the Tua river. The bridge over the river is a 15th-century construction, built on a Roman base. The old town of cobbled streets is dominated by the 17th-century town hall, home of the Távora family until the Marquês de Pombal had them all executed on a trumped up charge of treason. The modern Municipal Museum Armindo Teixeira Lopes (Museo Armindo Teixeira Lopes; Tue–Sun 9am–12.30pm and 2–5.30pm, Sat 2.30–6pm; free) and the Museum of Olive and Olive Oil (Museo da Oliveira e do Azeite; Tue–Sun 10am–6pm) are well worth a visit.

Halfway between Vila Real and Mirandela is the small town of **Murça**, most famous for its prehistoric carved stone pig, found on a platform in the main square.

Further south and east, in the Upper Douro region, the climate is noticeably warmer. The eccentrically named town of

Évora's Templo Romano

Freixo do Espada-à-Cinta ('Ash Tree of the Belted Sword') is where, according to legend, the 13th-century Dom Dinis hung his sword. He also built the town's seven-sided tower. The town has an enviable collection of Manueline buildings and attracts hordes of visitors during the spring to see flowering almond blossoms in the local orchards. The impressive Igreja de Matriz (the parish church) was rebuilt in 1520 in the Manueline style and has a magnificent painting attributed to Grão Vasco.

ALENTEJO

The 'land beyond the Tagus' (*alem Tejo* in Arabic) is a hot and dusty plain, sheathed in wheat, olive and cork trees, separating Lisbon from the Algarve. The Alentejo is one of Portugal's most fascinating and historic regions, nevertheless it frequently gets passed over by those hell-bent on getting to the southern beaches.

Although it accounts for approximately one third of the country's land area, these vast, sun-baked plains are sparsely populated. The slow-moving lifestyle has given rise to jokes about its equally slow inhabitants (such as the one about the Alentejano who keeps an empty bottle in the fridge for his friends who don't drink). The Alentejo is far more sophisticated and varied than it may first appear, with an excellent wine-making tradition, large aristocratic estates and some of the country's historic cities, such as Évora. Massive medieval fortresses stand watch atop steep hills along the Spanish border, and ancient dolmens – megalithic stones – dot the countryside. And for those who absolutely must see the Atlantic, the Alentejo has its own costa, the Costa Azul, or Blue Coast, a lower-key version of the Algarve.

ÉVORA

The acclaimed star of the Alentejo, **Évora** ⑱ (150km/93 miles east of Lisbon) was originally a Roman settlement and centre of learning. Today, it is a city of splendid Renaissance buildings, mostly dating from its heyday as the base of the House of Aviz (rulers of Portugal from the 14th century until the Spanish Habsburgs took over in 1581). By the 17th century, Évora had lost influence and development came to a halt, preserving the city's distinctive 16th-century *palácios* for posterity.

The major sights are enclosed within two rings of concentric walls and tucked among Évora's great maze of Moorish alleys and squares *(praças)*. The distinctive main square, **Praça do Giraldo**, is marked by Moorish arches and an attractive 16th-century fountain in its centre. The tourist office is located here.

Évora's **Templo Romano** (Roman Temple), sometimes called the Temple of Diana, dates to the 2nd or 3rd century AD. Its 14 Corinthian columns rise skyward from a platform that was in use as recently as the 19th century as a slaughterhouse.

Next to the Temple is the elegant **Pousada dos Lóios** (see page 186), a beautiful state-owned inn, formerly a convent. Abutting the *pousada* is the privately owned church of **São João Evangelista** (also known as Lóios, the old church of the same convent; Tue–Sun 10am–6pm). Inside are some of the country's finest examples of *azulejos*, created in the 18th century by the celebrated artist António Oliveira Bernardes, depicting the life of São Lourenço (St Lawrence). The church holds several other surprises. Hidden beneath trapdoors on either side of the aisle are a Moorish cistern 15m (50ft) deep and a collection of monks' bones, plus confession holes opening on to the *pousada's* cloister.

The fortress-like Romanesque style of the **Sé** (cathedral; Tue–Sun 9am–5pm; www.evoracathedral.com), begun in 1186, betrays its crusading origins. The impressive eastern wing was rebuilt by Johann Ludwig, the architect of the Convent at Mafra (see page 44), using the multicoloured marble of the Alentejo. The cathedral has an especially beautiful Gothic cloister and Sacred Art Museum, with an extraordinary impressive collection of relics and clerical vestments. The exquisitely carved upper choir has a Renaissance organ dating to 1562 – one of the oldest in Europe.

The **Igreja de São Fransisco** (daily 9am–5pm,

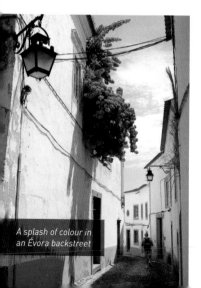

A splash of colour in an Évora backstreet

until 6.30pm in summer; charge for Capela dos Ossos; http://igrejadesaofrancisco. pt) holds one of Évora's greatest (and most maca-bre) attractions, the **Capela dos Ossos** (Chapel of Bones). The chapel is a large room wholly constructed with the bones of 5,000 monks; skulls form the window frames and femurs cover the col-umns. Over the entrance is a spooky sign that reminds visitors of their own mor-

> **Megalith mystery**
>
> The origins of Portugal's megaliths near Évora have been dated by archaeolo-gists to between the 5th and 3rd century BC. Although their exact purpose remains unknown, many experts have asserted that dolmens served as burial chambers and demarcated territories. At least 125 megalithic monuments have been found in the Alentejo.

tality: *Nós ossos que aqui estamos, Pelos vossos esperamos* ('We bones that are here, await the arrival of yours').

The **Museu de Évora** (Tue 2–6pm, Wed–Sun 10am–6pm), not far from the cathedral, is housed in the old archbishop's pal-ace. Extensive renovation shows off this important collection of paintings by the Flemish-inspired 'Portuguese School', the finest being a polyptych of 13 panels depicting the *Life of the Virgin* from the early 15th to late 16th century. The altarpiece was removed from the Sé in 1717.

EXCURSIONS FROM ÉVORA

The fine whitewashed town of **Arraiolos**, 21km (13 miles) north of Évora, is famed for its carpet workshops. The town's handwoven **wool rugs**, in the Moorish-Persian style, have been made here since the 17th century. While they aren't cheap (though less expensive than elsewhere), they are extremely beautiful.

Another excellent day trip from Évora is to the **megaliths** near **Reguengos de Monsaraz** (36km/22 miles to the south-east). These baffling prehistoric monuments, or dolmens, consist of standing stones (menhirs) and stone circles (cromlechs). Ask the tourist office in Évora for a pamphlet on these and other dolmens in the area, as well as for precise directions.

Near the Spanish border is **Monsaraz**, a quietly stunning fortified hilltop village with cobbled streets and spectacular views over the plains. The castle (occasionally hosting bull-fights) is one in the long chain of fortifications built by Dom Dinis in the 14th century.

THE MARBLE TOWNS

About 46km (28 miles) northeast of Évora, marble supplants more mundane building materials used for churches and palaces, thanks to the great number of quarries found at Estremoz, Borba and Vila Viçosa.

The largest of these quarries is near **Estremoz**, a walled town full of gleaming white marble stretching above the plains. The **Rossio** (Praça Marquês de Pombal) hosts the region's liveliest Saturday market, selling the famous pottery of Estremoz, tasty local cheese and other regional products. Also here is the tourist office and the beautiful marble-faced **Câmara Municipal** (town hall), which has impressive *azulejo* panels. About 400 metres away from the Rossio is the interesting **Museu Rural da Casa do Povo** (Rural Museum; daily 9am–12.30pm and 2–5.30pm; free), located in the Palácio dos Marqueses da Praia e Monforte, which displays a wealth of idiosyncratic local gadgets and pottery.

The upper town is reached through medieval walls. At the highest point is the 13th-century **Torre das Três Coroas** (castle keep, or Tower of Three Crowns), visible for miles around. Inside is the *azulejo*-covered chapel of Rainha Santa Isabel,

Tranquil Estremoz

dedicated to the memory of Dom Dinis's sainted queen. To one side is the white-marble Royal Palace, now part of one of the country's finest and most sought-after *pousadas*.

Borba, on the road to Elvas and Spain, is more down-to-earth, though marble buildings betray the source of its wealth: quarrying marble, as well as producing fine red and white wines. Every November the town hosts a wine festival.

Just up the road, 6km (4 miles) away, is a third marble town, **Vila Viçosa** ⑲. The pretty town is most remarkable for its impressive 16th-century **Paço Ducal** (Ducal Palace; Tue 2–5pm, until 6pm in summer, Wed–Sun 10am–1pm and 2–5pm, until 6pm in summer; last entry an hour before closing; www.cm-vilavicosa.pt) of the Bragança family, the last of Portugal's royal dynasties. The Paço used to be the Braganças' favourite country house, as they often preferred hunting in the enormous surrounding park to the fuss of Lisbon or the cold of their palace in Bragança. The

Vila Viçosa detail

guided tour (in English at 11am) provides an intimate glimpse of the royal apartments as they would have appeared before the assassination of Carlos I in 1908. Next door is the *pousada*, in a gorgeously restored 16th-century convent. The Bragança's previous residence, the hilltop castle, houses archaeological and hunting museums.

Further east, and nearer to Spain, is the mighty frontier fortress town of **Elvas**. The castle walls – among the best-preserved in Portugal – were modernised in the 17th century and given the characteristic star shape that distinguishes the work of Vauban, the French military architect.

Extending from the city's walls is the **Aqueduto da Amoreira**, an aqueduct some 7km (4 miles) long that took 124 years to complete. The town's largest church, on Praça da República, is the richly painted **Nossa Senhora da Assunção**, with an elaborate Manueline portal and bell tower overlooking the square. **Nossa Senhora dos Aflitos**, another church closer to the castle, has an octagonal shape, reflecting the influence of the Knights Templar, and its dome is covered in beautiful 17th-century *azulejos*.

NORTHEASTERN ALENTEJO

Portalegre is the prosperous, no-nonsense capital of the northern Alentejo, located near the hills and neolithic monuments of the Serra de São Mamede, 59km (36 miles) north of Estremoz. Its past wealth, based on carpet and silk production, accounts for the graceful 18th-century mansions lining the Rua 19 de Junho. By far the most interesting sight in town, though, is the **Museu da Tapeçaria de Portalegre Guy Fino** (Tue–Sun 9am–1pm and 2–6pm), showcasing pieces from the local tapestry factory, which creates amazing designs via a unique weaving method.

Alter do Chão (33km/20 miles southwest of Portalegre) is the location of the **Coudelaria de Alter Real** (Royal Stud Farm; guided visits only; Tue–Sun visits (groups of up to 8 people) at 11am and 3 pm; www.alterreal.pt), where Portugal's finest horses are bred. In the morning you can watch the Lusitanian and Alter do Chão horses being fed. There is also a museum containing armour and carriages, and the town has a fine restored castle.

Flôr da Rosa and **Crato** are two small agricultural towns west of Portalegre. In the former is one of the best examples of how the state *pousada* chain is adapting modern architecture to historic buildings. The inn now occupying the 14th-century **Convento de Flôr da Rosa** is extraordinary. Outside of town, on the road to Aldeia da Mata, is one of the best-preserved **dolmens** in Portugal, a mysterious prehistoric chamber sitting unobtrusively in rolling pastoral lands. In Crato is a stately square with an interesting **Varanda do Grão Prior**, with stone arches under a terrace once used for outdoor Mass, and a municipal museum of local handicrafts and artefacts two doors down. Above the town are the curious ruins of the castle, much amended by restoration.

North of Portalegre is the pleasant town of **Castelo da Vide**, whose 14th-century castle is surrounded by gleaming houses that nuzzle against the steeply sloping hill. Further down the hill, the winding alleyways of the **Judiaria** (Jewish Quarter) have survived and make a great place for a wander. Here is the country's oldest surviving synagogue (dating from the 13th century). For centuries, the fresh springs at **Fonte da Vila** have been an attraction, close to the handsome main square, the Praça Dom Pedro V.

A steep winding road leads to the dramatically situated medieval walled village of **Marvão ⓴**. Perched on an outcrop overlooking Spain, the easygoing town is the highest in Portugal (at 862m/2,800ft). The 13th-century castle walls appear woven right into the rock; the views from the ramparts of the whitewashed town and surrounding area are stunning. Marvão has almost all the charm of Óbidos (see page 45), but without the polish or tour bus crowds. Just outside the castle entrance is a handsome **Museu Municipal** (Tue–Sun 10am–12.30pm and 1.30–5pm), with interesting archaeological finds, religious artefacts and altarpieces and regional costumes.

BAIXO (LOWER) ALENTEJO

Of Roman origin (it was a regional capital under Julius Caesar), the agricultural city of **Beja** (78km/48 miles south of Évora) is at the hub of roads leading to Lisbon and the Algarve, and across the Alentejo. The old town is particularly attractive.

The decoratively crenellated **Torre de Menagem** (daily Apr–Oct 9.30am–noon and 2–4.30pm; Apr–Oct 9.30am–noon and 2–5.30pm) in the castle dates to the 13th century and provides a good lookout over extensive wheat fields. The city's most interesting sight is the **Convento da Nossa Senhora da Conceição** (Tue–Sun 9am–12.30pm and 2–5pm; www.museuregionaldebeja.pt; free on Sun), as it has fine Manueline carvings, bright Moorish-style *azulejos*, a splendid baroque chapel and an explosion of rococo gold leaf. The former convent houses

Marvão's medieval castle

an interesting regional museum with a good archaeological and painting collection. Another branch of the museum is the unique **Núcleo Visigótico** (Visigothic; same hours as above) in Santo Amaro, Beja's oldest church. The Pousada de São Francisco has been admirably converted from another convent, which was once derelict.

The charming, sleepy town of **Serpa** rises neatly above the plains, 30km (18 miles) east of Beja, on the route to Spain. Beyond the formidable Porta da Beja, a monumental gate in the city wall, small streets wend among bright white houses. Many of the buildings hide small cheese factories, which produce Serpa's well-known ewe's milk cheese. The town's castle was partially destroyed by a Spanish attack in 1707, but still affords enjoyable views. The walls continue past a privately owned 17th-century mansion and on to a slender aqueduct, which ends in an ancient well.

From Serpa a rewarding drive takes you south through a hilly and sparsely populated landscape, dotted with sheep. You can stop at **Mértola**, an ancient whitewashed town founded by the Phoenicians, built up by the Romans and later seized by the Moors. Perched on a ridge above the River Guadiana, the town is protected by Moorish walls and topped by a rather dilapidated castle with a profusion of storks' nests.

Mértola is steeped in history: its church, the **Igreja Matriz**, betrays a previous incarnation as a mosque with a prayer niche (mihrab), while the town hall is constructed on Roman foundations (now a museum; Tue–Sun 9.15am–12.30pm and 4–5.15pm). The Guadiana River continues to the Algarve, forming part of the border with Spain. The road that follows it is one of the most beautiful routes between the Alentejo and the Algarve.

Painted chairs for sale

COASTAL ALENTEJO

The Alentejo coast, a popular holiday destination with the Portuguese, has a character slightly different from that of the even more popular Algarve. The water here is colder and the winds and waves greater, but it is also noticeably quieter, more relaxed and less expensive. Often the best beaches are those near a river estuary, thus giving visitors the choice of surfing in the Atlantic or swimming in the calmer waters of the river.

The northernmost point of the coastal Alentejo is the narrow, sandy peninsula of **Tróia**, 46km (28 miles) northwest of the attractive town of Alcácer do Sal. Tróia has beaches on both the Sado estuary and the ocean, but the town

> ### Windmill towers
>
> Scattered about the surrounding hills is a profusion of windmill towers which, without their white canvas sails, look for all the world like ancient cannons.

has been heavily developed in recent years to accommodate ferries from Setúbal. Even so, it is worth visiting the remains of the Roman fishing village of Cetobriga. You can escape the crowds on the beaches of the ocean side.

Further to the south and slightly inland is the town of **Santiago do Cacém**, hemmed in by low-lying hills on three sides and crowned by a hilltop castle, which holds a macabre cemetery full of disinterred bones. The lagoons of **Santo André** and **Melides** are both easily accessible from the town and have long stretches of beach, sea and lagoon swimming, as well as small beachside communities.

THE ALGARVE

To many international visitors, the Algarve is Portugal, but the Portuguese see the Algarve as an anomaly. The area's distinctive character owes much to its strong Moorish heritage, many spectacular beaches and Mediterranean climate, so different from most other parts of the country.

The region's popularity with millions of holiday-makers has produced an explosion of purpose-built holiday villages which have given rise to many excellent sporting facilities, and there are still some quiet and untouristy areas. Access from one part

The Algarve is popular for its golden beaches

to another is along the EN125 road, which runs most of the length of the coast.

The Sotavento Coast, beween Faro and Spain, is made up of salt marshes and lagoons, with beautiful sandy beaches on the barrier islands just offshore. The most intensively developed part stretches westward from Faro to Portimão. The more dramatic Barlavento Coast extends west from Portimão, and is characterised by a twisting shoreline indented with coves and wind-sculpted cliffs. The coast comes to an end at Cabo de São Vicente, known to the medieval Portuguese as the End of the World. The west coast is wilder, colder, windier and considerably emptier, even though it has its fair share of wonderful beaches. Inland you'll find Roman and Moorish monuments, orchards and the scenic wooded hillsides of the *serras* that separate the Algarve from the Alentejo.

BARLAVENTO COAST

The town of **Sagres** and the area around it are remote, rugged and weathered, with only a relative smattering of hotels, restaurants and other facilities aimed at tourists. It is like the Algarve's outpost, which is precisely why it has so many admirers. The town has a picturesque working harbour and a quaint little square, Praça da República, and, in summer, some lively nightspots.

Prince Henry the Navigator established an informal, but renowned, centre of research here, where he invited assorted specialists – mathematicians, cartographers, experienced sea captains, wealthy traders and more – to gather their knowledge and ideas in the cause of advancing exploration. He collected books, maps, charts and pilots' manuals, helped by his brother Pedro, also a keen traveller.

Prince Henry himself, with memories of his childhood in Porto and of the Douro port-carrying *barcos*, is credited with designing the easy-to-sail caravel. However, historians are uncertain where Henry actually lived. He was often in Lagos – from where he sailed to Ceuta in an expeditionary fleet of conquest, his only sea voyage. He had lodgings in Raposeira. He worked from a Vila do Infante, its location unknown. With its geographical allure, its fort and restored wind rose, or compass rose, it was Sagres that came to signify the launch of the Age of Discovery.

The best beaches near Sagres – **Mareta**, **Martinhal**, **Beliche**, **Tonel** and **Telheiro** – are sheltered and not overcrowded. Beyond Sagres, a great, rocky peninsula hangs above a brooding ocean. Henry and his sailors are popularly believed to have set up camp at the **Fortaleza de Sagres** (fortress) that sits on the promontory, though little of the original structure has survived. Inside is a small 16th-century chapel, Nossa Senhora da Graça, and the huge stone **Rosa dos Ventos** (wind rose or compass rose).

A couple of kilometres (1 mile) west of Sagres are the remains of another fortress, **Fortaleza do Beliche**. At the tip of the windswept cliffs of **Cabo de São Vicente**, the lighthouse, built in 1904 on the site of a convent chapel, has a beam visible up to 96km (60 miles) away.

Lagos ㉑, the principal resort of the western Algarve, is the rare beach town that offers something for everyone. By night Lagos is lively, with outdoor restaurant terraces and bars,

⊙ A WEALTH OF PRODUCE

Trees bear a wealth of produce for Portugal. Fruit is abundant – apples, oranges and succulent Elvas plums grow in the Algarve. Olive trees daub great stretches of landscape in soft grey-green. Almonds are everywhere, the blossom – Algarve's 'winter snow' – is a perennial delight. Chestnuts are in the north, eucalyptus across many hillsides. The tall carob tree, *alfarrobeira*, produces a long black bean from whose seeds came the word 'carat'. It's in health foods, ice cream – and reportedly fed the Duke of Wellington's horses in his campaign against Napoleon.

Cork oaks, their bark used as floats by ancient Egyptians, have a thousand uses from insulation to wall decoration to shoes to bottle stoppers. Producers, concerned at the increasing trend toward screwtops, are developing new techniques to perfect standard corks. Portugal's cork industry, all the same, remains the world's biggest, producing for champagne alone some 500 million bottle corks a year. Watertight, without odour or taste, cork – carefully cut from trees every nine or so years – has a versatility no synthetic product can match.

and by day it combines a rich historical past with a busy present. Attractive beaches are on the outskirts of town, so it is not a classic resort in the mould of Praia da Rocha.

The restored fortress, **Forte da Ponte da Bandeira**, guarded the harbour entrance in the 17th century. Many of the streets are narrow, cobbled and built for donkeys rather than hire cars. Though Lagos town

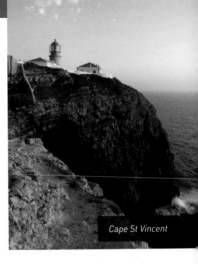

Cape St Vincent

still retains a good part of its original walls – most of them from the 16th century, but part-Roman in places – they have been rebuilt and expanded over the centuries. Lagos was an important trading port under the Moors, but had its heyday after the Reconquest, when it briefly became both the military and civil capital of the Algarve. Its slave market building is still standing.

On Rua General Alberta da Silveira, **Igreja de Santo António**, an exuberant gilt baroque chapel and one of the Algarve's finest churches, was rebuilt soon after the 1755 earthquake. The entrance to the church is through the delightfully eclectic museum next door, **Museu Municipal** (Tue–Sun 10am–12.30pm and 2–5.30pm). Rooms display sacred art, archaeological remains, the original charter of Lagos and a bizarre collection of creatures: for example, an eight-legged goat kid preserved in formaldehyde, a one-eyed sheep and a cat with two faces.

Ponta da Piedade, a photographer's delight

The main street of Lagos is the charming, cobbled **Rua 25 de Abril**, packed with restaurants, bars and ceramics shops. The beaches near Lagos range from **Meia Praia**, 1.6km (1 mile) to the east, a long (4km/2 miles) flat stretch, to pocket-sized coves just west of the city. **Praia de Dona Ana** and **Praia do Camilo** are both small, pretty and crowded. Weird and wonderful rock formations and steep cliffs that glow orange at sunset are popular with photographers; **Ponta da Piedade** (Point of Piety) at the southern tip, before the road turns west to Sagres, is part of a stack and cliff formation, a stunning terracotta sequence of bridges, terraces and grottoes.

PORTIMÃO TO FARO

Portimão, second only to Faro in size in the Algarve, is the most businesslike town on the coast. But nestled around it are some of the Algarve's finest beaches, which have transformed the area into one of the coast's most popular resorts. Praia da Rocha and Praia Três Irmãos in particular are packed with hotels and beach-goers. Most of Portimão's local colour is down by the port, a haven of fishing activity.

The top fish-canning spot on the Algarve, Portimão is renowned for its restaurants specialising in *sardinhas assadas* (grilled sardines). In the centre of town, **Largo 1 de Dezembro** is a 19th-century park with 10 splendid blue-and-white *azulejo* benches, each illustrating a pivotal event in the history of Portugal. Along Rua Machado dos Santos is the handsome **Igreja da Nossa Senhora da Conceição**, with steps up to it. The yellow and white church, constructed in the 15th century, has a beautiful Gothic portico with carved capitals, though it looks colonial as a result of its reconstruction in the 18th and 19th centuries.

From the centre of town, head to the waterfront, especially if it's near lunch or dinner time. You can almost follow your nose towards the aroma of grilled sardines, which will lead you to the **dockside**, lined with simple restaurants all serving delicious, smoky sardines and other freshly caught fish.

Just 3km (2 miles) down river is **Praia da Rocha**, which became a holiday village for wealthy Portuguese families at the end of the 19th century. The British came in the 1930s, when this 2km (1-mile) golden 'beach of rocks' provided an inspirational refuge for writers and intellectuals. The beach also attracts divers who flock to the **Ocean Revival Underwater Park** (www.oceanrevival.org), the largest artificial reef in the world made up of four scuttled warships. At the eastern end, guarding the River Arade, is the **Fortaleza de Santa Catarina de Ribamar** (St Catherine's Fortress), built in 1621 to defend Silves and Portimão against attack. It has a view over the estuary.

The opposite end of Praia da Rocha's long stretch is known as **Praia do Vau.** The splendid rock formations and coves continue, but this part is quieter and less developed.

Just west, **Praia de Três Irmãos** ㉒ is the slightly upmarket cousin of Praia da Rocha. At the eastern end of the beach is a beautiful cove, hemmed in by cliffs and ochre rocks. Beyond it, the beach stretches to **Alvor,** a classic Algarvian fishermen's village, where narrow cobbled streets plunge downhill to a quay and market, and boats bob on a marshy lagoon.

North of Portimão, the **Serra de Monchique** mountain range extends westward, dividing the coast from the hot plains. The *serra* is covered with cork, pine and chestnut trees, and wild flowers.

The first stop on the scenic journey along route 266 is the spa village of **Caldas de Monchique,** known since Roman times for its therapeutic waters. North of Caldas, the road weaves uphill quickly, rising 300m (1,000ft) in 5km (3 miles) past terraced farmlands and forests. **Monchique** is a small market town, known for its handicrafts and the famous Manueline portico of its 16th-century **Igreja Matriz.**

The road continues upwards, towards **Fóia,** almost 902m (3,000ft) above sea level. On a clear day you can see from the bay of Portimão to the Sagres peninsula and pick out the rocky outcrops on the Lagos beaches.

Silves ㉓ is the former Moorish capital of the Algarve. More than eight centuries ago, Silves, as Chelb, was one of the strongest outposts in 12th-century Arabic Iberia, a magnificent city of palaces, gardens, bazaars and a huge red castle on a hill.

Silves is now a charming backwater, but the glorious setting remains. The imposing, rust-red **Castelo dos Mouros** (Moors' Castle; daily 9am–5.30pm) took shape after the Reconquest,

A tranquil scene at the busy resort of Praia da Rocha

though it preserves distinctly Moorish lines. Next to the castle is the impressive Gothic **Sé Velha** (Old Cathedral; Mon–Fri 9am–1pm, 2–6pm, Sat 9am–1pm), built by the liberating Christian crusaders. Opposite the Sé is the 16th-century **Igreja da Misericórdia** with a classic Manueline-style side door. The imposing **Torreão da Porta da Cidade** (Turret of the City Gate) shows the importance given to Silves' defence.

The attractive resort of **Carvoeiro**, an archetypal small Barlavento resort, has a tiny beach at the bottom of a pretty valley. Although the original village is now fairly commercialised, it hasn't lost its appeal.

Inland, just off the main road, is the pleasant little village of **Porches ㉔**, with some classic, white Algarve houses and filigreed chimneys. Porches is famous for **handpainted pottery**, though you won't find much in the village. Large outlets for these distinctive ceramics can be found along the N125.

One of the most photographed beaches on this stretch is **Nossa Senhora da Rocha** (Our Lady of the Rock). The rock boldly juts out into the sea, surmounted by a little white fishermen's church. The beach of **Armação de Pêra** is one of the longest in the Algarve but the massive development at the eastern end has pretty much ruined the area's natural beauty.

Albufeira, at one time a picturesque fishermen's town, has grown wildly in recent years to become the leading resort in the Algarve. Its clifftop position and labyrinthine street plan provided an easily defensible spot for the Moors, and Albufeira proved one of the last towns to fall during the Reconquest.

Modern Albufeira has fallen prey to mass tourism, with bars, cafés and nightspots pumping out music day and night, but the excellent beaches west of town are relatively uncrowded. The best are **São Rafael** and **Coelha**, **Castelo** and Galé, three small, beautiful coves.

One of the most picturesque towns in the province is the lovely village **Alte**, about 30km (18 miles) north of Albufeira. The architectural highlight is the beautiful 16th-century Igreja Matriz, entered through a classic Manueline portal. The rest of Alte is the Algarve of picture postcards – whitewashed houses, narrow streets, colourful windows, filigreed chimney pots.

Loosely grouped with Albufeira are beaches to the east. Here on the coastline is the last of the dramatic rock formations that have made the Algarve so famous. **Falésia** is a beautiful beach framed by high cliffs, but to get to it you need to negotiate the grounds of the Sheraton Algarve, whose elevator down to the beach is for guests only. There are more excellent beaches at **Santa Eulalia, Balaia**, **Praia da Oura** and **São João**. The centre of activity along this beach hinterland is the infamous 'strip' in the form of a long street of bustling bars, restaurants and nightspots leading up to the hilltop area known as Montechoro.

A view over Silves with the Old Cathedral in the distance

Next along the coast is **Vilamoura**, a completely planned and sanitised tourist undertaking with high-rise hotels and sprawling villas that line manicured golf courses to the 19th-hole club bar and the Algarve's biggest marina. It's a major draw for golfers; several of the Algarve's best courses are here.

A little further east, **Quarteira**, once a quiet fishing village, is today virtually unrecognisable, subsumed under an onslaught of rows and rows of apartment buildings. But the terrain soon begins to change when the rugged, rocky lines of the Barlavento coast give way to long flat beaches.

The small crossroads town of **Almancil** has shops, cafés and businesses, many of which are dedicated to serving English expatriates. Back on the coast are two of the Algarve's most luxurious and exclusive resorts, **Vale do Lobo**, a maze-like villa community with a good long beach and a variety of golf and tennis resort hotels, and **Quinta do Lago**, which has one of the finest golf courses in the Algarve, designed with some care along the **Ria Formosa Nature Reserve**. The beach can be reached across a wooden bridge that crosses over wetlands and bird sanctuaries.

Back toward Almancil is one of the Algarve's top attractions. About 16km (10 miles) west of Faro, a simple white church stands out on a small hill overlooking the thundering highway. A sign simply says 'S. Lourenço' – indicating the turn-off to **São Lourenço dos Matos** (Church of St Lawrence of the Woods). Inside is one of the most extraordinary displays of *azulejo* design you'll ever see. Every square inch of the baroque, 15th-century church – its walls, vaulted ceiling and cupola – is covered with hand-painted, blue-and-white ceramic tiles. Most date from the early 18th century and depict biblical scenes detailing the life of St Lawrence.

Loulé, north of Almancil, is a prosperous town known for its leather, lace and copper goods. People come from far and wide to shop at the colourful, bustling market. Just below the permanent market halls on the main Praça da República, you'll find a well-preserved section of the medieval castle walls (which were much damaged by the 1755 earthquake). Also worth visiting are the **Igreja Matriz** (São Clemente), a 13th-century Gothic church with 18th-century *azulejo* tiles; the **Convento da Graça**, with a superb Manueline portal; and **Ermida de Nossa Senhora da Conceição**, a small church prized for its baroque altar and tiles. In the streets below the castle walls, you may hear the sound of craftsmen beating copper into utensils that you can buy directly from them.

São Brás de Alportel is another market town and site of one of three comfortable *pousadas* (inns) along the Algarve, in the midst of

Algarve fishermen

Fishermen of the Algarve have a long history. In 1353 Edward III, King of England, gave them the right to fish off the coast of England.

Ria Formosa Nature Reserve

rolling orchards of fig, olive and orange trees. The **Museu do Traje** (Museum of Costumes; Mon–Fri 10am–1pm and 2–5pm, Sat–Sun 2–5pm; www.museu-sbras.com) has exhibits of local dress in a large, old house 90m (100yds) off the main square.

On the road to Faro, the **Palácio de Estói** 25 is a most curious find. The attractive 18th-century rococo palace once belonged to the Dukes of Estói. It's been converted into a luxurious *pousada*. Its **gardens** are an intriguing sight with balustrade terraces and staircases with splendid bursts of bougainvillea, busts of historic characters impaled on the parapets, brightly coloured wall tiles and formal gardens.

The **Vila Romana de Milreu** (Tue–Sun, May–Sept 9.30am–1pm and 2–6.30pm, Oct–Apr 9.30am–1pm and 2–5.30pm) is 1.5km (1 mile) down the road from Estói towards Faro. A small sign on the side of the road reads 'Ruinas de Milreu' (ruins of Milreu). The tall, semi-circular ruin of a Roman tower is thought to have been a temple to pagan water gods at one time; however, by the 5th century it had clearly been converted to a church. The Roman mosaics, though small, are impressive.

FARO

Faro 26, the provincial capital of the Algarve, is bypassed by many tourists, though the town has a greater wealth of cultural and historic monuments than any other Algarve town, as well as a picturesque old quarter.

At the main entrance to the circular Vila-Adentro (historic centre), near the harbour, stands the 19th-century **Arco da Vila**, a lovely arch and bell tower on which storks tend to nest. Beyond

⊙ NATIONAL PARKS AND PROTECTED AREAS

The map of Portugal, from south to north, is patched with a considerable range of environmental special cases, classified variously as parks, reserves and protected areas. Around Faro in the south is the Ria Formosa (meaning the Lovely Lagoon) with gorgeous islands, beaches and birds. The Algarve's west coast is a wild place of dramatic craggy cliffs and infinite beaches. The Tagus and Sado estuaries are equally rich in birdlife, waders especially. Sintra and Cascais, both heavily visited, definitely need loving care. On the Berlenga Islands you can camp close to nesting seabirds. Dinosaur footprints inland hint at Portugal's prehistory. The stunning Serra da Estrela, mountains of the stars, are not so much about height but beauty – and snowy slopes, even skiing, in winter. The two most northern parks, Montesinho and Peneda-Gerês, are thrilling landscapes, at times pretty chilly, and great for walking.

the arch, a cobbled street, polished by centuries of tramping feet, leads up to the splendid expanse of the **Largo da Sé** (Cathedral Square) – best seen by evening floodlight.

São Lourenço dos Matos

The **Sé**'s unusual tower, main portico and two interior chapels are all that remain of the original 13th-century Gothic cathedral. Inside is one of the Algarve's most important collections of 17th- and 18th-century sacred art. Climb the **tower** (Mon–Fri 10am–6.30pm, Sat 9.30am–1pm) for fine views over the whole of Faro.

The **Convento de Nossa Senhora da Assunção** (Convent of Our Lady of the Assumption) was the first Renaissance building in the Algarve and it contains what is perhaps the most magnificent cloister in southern Portugal. It has been beautifully restored as the **Museu Municipal** (Oct–May Tue–Fri 10am–6pm, Sat–Sun 10am–5pm, June–Sept Tue–Fri 10am–7pm, Sat–Sun 11.30am–6pm; free on Sun until winter 2.30pm/summer 3.30pm) and its principal exhibit is an amazing 2,000-year-old Roman floor mosaic, 9m (30ft) long and 3m (10ft) wide.

Central Faro's main thoroughfare is Rua de Santo António. At its far end beside the Praça da Liberdade in a building that houses the District Assembly is the **Museu Regional do Algarve** (Tue–Fri 10am–6pm, Sat 10am–4.30pm) which includes reconstructions of rooms in a typical Algarve house. The museum sits on the edge

The macabre Capela dos Ossos

of Faro's Mouraria, or old Moorish quarter. The new town, an expansion dating from the 19th century, lies west of here. The **Igreja de São Pedro** (Church of St Peter), built in the 16th century, has a carved baroque retable and a couple of rococo chapels.

But Faro's finest church is **Igreja do Carmo** (Carmelite Church). The promise of its twin bell towers and stately façade is matched by a beautiful gilded interior, but more interesting is the macabre **Capela dos Ossos** (Chapel of Bones). This 19th-century curiosity, like a similar one in Évora (see page 97), is constructed of the skulls and bones of monks, unearthed from the friars' cemetery. Depending on your tolerance for such things, you'll find it either fascinating or horrible.

THE SOTAVENTO COAST

Heading east out of Faro, you will come to the colourful fishing town of **Olhão**, commonly described as the little white Cubist town of the Algarve because of the similarity of its architecture to that of North African towns. The parish church of **Nossa Senhora do Rosário** was founded by King Dom Pedro II in 1698. The small chapel at the rear, Nossa Senhora dos Aflitos (Our Lady of the Afflicted), is where women often pray when their fishermen husbands are away at sea.

Instead of the red-tiled roofs and filigreed chimneys seen elsewhere in the Algarve, the Olhão skyline comprises flat-topped roofs of terraces called *açoeitas*. The **Olhão fish market** is one of the Algarve's best, especially famous for its mussels and other shellfish.

With its Moorish, Reconquista and Renaissance roots clearly visible, **Tavira** ㉗ is one of the Algarve's most historically rich cities. In the 1500s, Tavira had the largest population in the region. This former tuna-fishing port full of historic churches, imposing classical-style mansions and beautiful riverfront gardens probably dates back at least as far as the Phoenicians or the Carthaginians. In fact, its seven-arched stone bridge of Roman origin is still in use.

Tavira's **castle**, in the centre of the *casco histórico* (old quarter), was a defensive structure built by the Moors. The walls look directly onto the **Igreja de Santa Maria do Castelo** (Church of St Mary of the Castle) whose Gothic portal is the only original 13th-century element of the building to have survived the devastating 1755 earthquake. Across the square, the ochre-coloured former convent, **Convento da Graça**, has been converted into a *pousada*.

Just down the hill, off Rua Galeria near the river, is the beautiful 16th-century **Igreja da Misericórdia** (Church of Mercy), a spectacular Renaissance edifice with a carved portico. **Rua da Liberdade**, Tavira's main street, is lined with stately 16th-century mansions.

A good excursion from Tavira is to the nearby island **Ilha de Tavira**, where

Loulé Carnival

If you are in the Algarve in springtime, don't miss the Loulé Carnival. The parades, 'Battle of Flowers' and musical celebrations are the best of their kind in the region.

Tavira blooms

there is a wonderful, huge beach backed by sand dunes. Ferries make the five-minute trip from Quatro Águas, a couple of kilometres (1 mile) east of the town (year-round) or from the river harbour in the town centre (summer). Back on the mainland, a turning off the main road (N125) leads to the uncrowded **Cacela Velha**, a perfectly enchanting little whitewashed village overlooking the sea. It has an 18th-century church, a telephone booth, a cemetery, an old well and some well tended blue-and-white houses festooned with flowers.

East of here lie the high-rise canyons of **Monte Gordo**. The raison d'être of all the development here is the long but not especially attractive sandy beach, which stretches undisturbed for some 10km (6 miles).

The Guadiana River, which flows into the Atlantic 3km (2 miles) east of Monte Gordo, served as a natural frontier for some 2,000 years, forming the boundary between the Roman provinces of

Lusitania (Portugal) and Baetica (southern Spain). This geographical context explains the strategic importance of **Castro Marim**, a fortress town occupied by the Moors for five centuries.

Back on the coast, the dignified town of **Vila Real de Santo António ㉘** (the Royal Town of St Anthony) is the last of the Algarve's beach towns before Spain. The town was built in just five months in 1774, copying the grid layout of Lisbon's Baixa (lower city). The **Praça do Marquês do Pombal**, is the tour de force of Vila Real, with black-and-white paving radiating from an obelisk in the centre of the square like rays from the sun. The town's main appeal is the ferry to the white town of **Ayamonte** across the water in Spain. The trip takes just 20 minutes – quicker than going over the bridge – but you will need to take your passport (or identification card in case of EU citizens). Note there is an hour's time difference between here and Spain.

THE WEST COAST

North from Sagres, along the west coast, is the one part of the Algarve that may well escape intensive development, simply because, although the beaches are broad and sandy and the coastline dramatic, the water is colder and the wind stronger. For those interested in surfing or solitude, this coast may prove to be ideal.

A ruined Moorish castle looks over the small town of **Aljezur**, which makes a good base. The Serra de Monchique is within striking distance, and the neighbouring beaches include the enormous rocky cove at **Arrifana** and the wider dune beach of **Monte Clérigo**. Both have small tourist complexes.

Further north, **Odeceixe** is a pretty village set in a small river valley, which continues down to a wide, cliff-backed beach at the estuary of the River Vascão.

Festa de São João illuminations, Évora

WHAT TO DO

With its agreeable climate as prime temptation, Portugal's long coast of splendid beaches and inland diversity – hills, mountains, plains, rivers – offer endless opportunities for relaxed or active pursuits. Meanwhile there's a rich cultural heritage to be found in every city, town and village. Portugal's open-hearted people, enthralling markets, savoury cooking and excellent wines should please the most demanding traveller.

SHOPPING

Though Portugal has malls and modern shops, its quaint old premises make it one of the most delightful countries in which to browse, especially in the major cities of Lisbon and Porto.

Traditional crafts are still practised. Intricate works of gold and silver, handpainted ceramics, basket work and classic wool rugs are sold in small shops and outdoor markets across the country. The best of the handicrafts are promoted through ventures such as the first floor of the Ribeira market in Lisbon. There are, of course, chic fashion and jewellery boutiques, too, particularly in Lisbon, Porto and the Algarve, as well as cellars stocking port

Tax tip

For non-EU residents, the IVA tax (Value Added Tax) imposed on most goods can be refunded on major purchases. Look for the blue-and-white TAX FREE sign in stores and fill out a form provided by the shop when you are buying your goods. The refund can be credited to your credit card at the airport or sent to you after your return.

Feira da Ladra, Lisbon

wine and other excellent wines. Many consumer goods remain inexpensive in the smaller towns.

WHAT TO BUY

Brass, bronze and copper. Candlesticks, pots and pans, old-fashioned scales, bowls and trays can be found across Portugal. *Cataplanas* make a delightful decorative or functional souvenir. The Moorish tradition of producing cooking utensils from beaten metal is maintained in the town of Loulé, in the Algarve.

Carpets and rugs. Attractive and excellently crafted hand-made rugs, mostly from the Alentejo region, have been produced for centuries. Arraiolos wool rugs are colourful and rustic-looking; the small town of the same name has a few dozen small dealers.

Ceramics, pottery and azulejos. Portugal is renowned for its colourful and handpainted glazed pottery and tiles. You can buy a single blue-and-white tile, an address plaque for your house, or an entire set of plates. Some shops will paint tiles to order or copy a photograph. Ceramics can be heavy and fragile to carry home; ask about shipping options. Each region has its own distinctive style, ranging from the intricately painted *faience* animals of Coimbra to the roosters of Barcelos and the black pottery of Chaves. Good places to buy are the Azulejo Museum in Lisbon and the shops along the N125 in the Algarve. Porches has two major outlets: Olaria Algarve (Porches Pottery), which has revived and updated old Moorish styles, and Casa Algarve.

Cork. Portugal is the world's leading producer of cork. You'll find place mats, intricate sculptures and other designs, and it's as light as a feather to take home.

Embroidery. A great many embroidered items, including tablecloths and napkins, are available all over Portugal – especially at street markets. Look for the delicate needlework that comes from the island of Madeira – items that are exceedingly well crafted but still comparatively inexpensive.

Jewellery. Filigree work, a legacy of the Moors, is of high quality. Look for silver filigree earrings and brooches, often in the form of flowers or butterflies.

Leather. You can find a good selection of fashionable, inexpensive shoes, belts and handbags, as well as jackets, wallets and gloves. Lisbon has many shoe emporia in the Baixa.

Music. Take home the sounds of Portugal on a classic *fado* recording, or some traditional music played on some of Portugal's unique instruments.

Sweet gifts

Even if you don't devour them all yourself you might consider the Algarve-made marzipan sweets, shaped and coloured like mini-vegetables, as a gift to take home.

Wine and food. Wine from the Dão, Douro, Minho and Alentejo travels well, but nothing carries quite as well as port. The best places to buy are the major producers' cellars in Vila Nova de Gaia. Cured sausages keep a while, too, and sweets and candies made from almonds, marzipan and figs also make very good gifts to take home.

WHEN AND WHERE TO SHOP

Most shops are open at least Monday–Friday 9am–1pm and 3–7pm and Saturday 9am–1pm. Modern shopping malls are usually open 10am–midnight or later, and often on Sunday as well. Increasingly, shops also stay open during lunchtime. Country markets start business at around 8am and continue until mid-afternoon.

Street markets (*feiras* or *mercados*) are fun for their atmosphere, and the goods for sale include all kinds of crafts, clothing and food items. In Lisbon, behind São Vicente de Fora church, the Feira da Ladra ('Thieves' Market') is held on Tuesday and Saturday. Barcelos holds the country's largest weekly market. The National Craft Fair in Vila do Conde, near Porto (July and August), and the Craft Fair in Lagoa in the Algarve (August), both display crafts from all over the country.

Major credit cards are accepted in almost all shops in the cities, but less so in the smaller towns. Prices are generally fixed, except in markets, where you can bargain.

> ### Shopping centres
>
> Smart, well-stocked malls, with multiplex cinemas, are to be found in the major cities and towns. Lisbon's huge Colombo shopping centre (www. colombo.pt) has instant Metro access from the Colégio Militar station.

ENTERTAINMENT

Night entertainment options differ greatly depending on where you are. Lisbon and Porto offer all kinds of live music, theatre, bars and clubs, and the Algarve resorts are well-stocked with bars and discos. Smaller towns tend to be much quieter.

Shopping for hats in Amarante

Fado. The classic night out in Lisbon still belongs to the *fado* houses *(casas de fado)* in Alfama or Bairro Alto. Many offer dinner as well as drinks. *Fado*'s origins are unclear; it may have developed as a form of mourning for men lost at sea or it may be a relic of the days of slavery–a kind of Iberian blues. Typically a *fado* troupe consists of a woman dressed in black accompanied by a couple of men playing the 12-stringed Portuguese guitar and what they call a viola, or Spanish guitar. The music is a swell of longing, regret and nostalgia and much too solemn to dance to, so regional dances may also be performed to perk things up. Lisbon *fado* houses to consider include: **Adega Machado** (Rua do Norte, 91; www.adegamachado.pt); **A Parreirinha da Alfama** (Beco do Espírito Santa, 1; www.parrei rinhadealfama.com); **A Severa** (Rua das Gáveas, 51; www.asevera. com); and **Senhor Vinho** (Rua do Meio à Lapa; www.srvinho.com).

Along the Algarve, you'll also find 'fado nights' at bars and hotels, where you can get the flavour of this quintessentially Portuguese musical expression.

Other live music and performing arts. Lisbon is home to a wide range of opera, ballet and classical concerts. The city's opera company is highly regarded and the Gulbenkian Foundation maintains its own symphony orchestra and choir company. The national ballet company has a new home in the Parque das Nações. Porto also has state-of-the-art concert halls and theatres. The Algarve maintains an orchestra with full programmes throughout the country.

Nightclubs. Lisbon and Porto are both packed with clubs and bars that go late into the night. In Lisbon, Bairro Alto is the centre of the bar action, but the former docks at Alcântara are also lively, while clubbers in Porto often head for Foz do Douro. Popular Algarve resorts such as Albufeira and Praia da Rocha throb to the latest dance anthems, while Lagos is a great place

A traditional fado troupe

to party away the summer, attracting a mixed crowd. Évora and Coimbra are university towns, dotted with bars and clubs. Most other towns are relatively quiet at night.

Gambling. The main casino in Lisbon is in Estoril, which has helped make the resort famous. Its operators have also been granted a licence to build a casino in the capital on the fashionable riverside Jardim do Tobaco. Another casino, Casino de Lisboa, is located in the Parque das Nações in the Auditorio dos Oceanos (tel: 218 929 000, www.casino-lisboa.pt/). Casinos are also found in the Algarve at Monte Gordo, Vilamoura and Praia da Rocha, as well as at Figueira da Foz, Espinho and Póvoa de Varzim. You must be over 21 and carry a passport.

SPORTS

Sports enthusiasts have plenty of options in Portugal. The temperate climate in the south also means year-round golf and tennis.

WATER SPORTS

Diving and snorkelling. There are some three dozen centres along Portugal's long southern coastline that cater to divers. It is especially popular in the western Algarve at Luz, Lagos and Sagres. Along the Estoril Coast and just off Sesimbra, south of Lisbon, the extraordinarily clear, calm waters provide excellent snorkelling and scuba diving.

Fishing. All along the coast you will see anglers in boots casting off from the beaches, and others perched on rocks or man-made promontories. A permit is required for river and lake fishing; details are available from branches of the Portuguese National Tourist Office (see page 176) or the Instituto Florestal (Avenida João Crisóstomo 26, 1000 Lisbon).

Getting ready to sail in Cascais

Angling conditions are generally best in the winter from October to mid-January.

Boats can be rented in Portimão, Faro, Sesimbra or Setúbal along the Algarve. One of the best game fishing spots is around Sesimbra, known for its swordfish. The waters of the Algarve provide some of the best game fishing in Europe.

Sailing and boating. Most beaches protected from the open sea have rowing boats, canoes or pedalos for rent by the hour. Experienced sailors in search of a more seaworthy craft should ask at the local yacht harbour. In the Algarve, dinghies and sailing instruction are available at Praia de Luz, Quinta do Lago and Portimão. For bigger craft try the marina at Vilamoura or the Carvoeiro Club (www.carvoeirovillas.com). Cruises are available in virtually every settlement along the Algarve. You can also canoe along mountain rivers and reservoirs in northern Portugal, such as in the Minho.

Swimming. With great beaches all around the Portuguese coast, opportunities for swimming could not be better. The Algarve has warmer water and more sheltered beaches than the west coast. Lifeguards are not common. Most hotels have swimming pools. Because of pollution along the Estoril Coast, you should not swim any closer to Lisbon than at Estoril itself, which has been granted an EU blue flag (for safe conditions).

LAND SPORTS

Cycling. There are plenty of mountain-biking opportunities in northern Portugal, with activity companies offering myriad tours in the mountains, particularly around Parque Natural da Serra da Estrela; the 13km (8-mile) Ecopista is a scenic cycling trail above the Minho river.

Golf. Portugal is one of the world's top destinations for golfing holidays, with many companies offering all-inclusive holidays. There are immaculate courses around Lisbon, especially Estoril with its famous Golf do Estoril, which hosts the Open de Portugal. There are also a few near Porto, but it is the Algarve which has the lion's share. Particularly notable are those at Vilamoura and Quinta do Lago.

⊙ BEACHES: A DAZZLING CHOICE

While in Portugal you may want to go shopping, check out regional wines, play golf, visit a museum, birdwatch, explore a natural park, walk in the hills, go boating or fish from one of the marinas. But bear in mind that wherever you go in Portugal, and whatever you do, an abundance of stunning beaches is never far away. No more than 563km (350 miles) long and 225km (140 miles) wide, Atlantic-edged to the west and south, Portugal is fringed for almost its full length by gleaming white sand. In the south, the Algarve's Sotavento (the eastern coast) is long and alluring. From Faro to the southwest tip and up the west coast are shining coves and beaches, as popular as Albufeira's, as cosy as Carvoeiro's. From the Algarve's wilder west coast all the way to the north are a series of beaches, one more dazzling than the next, where quite often there's not a soul to be seen.

Request a brochure from a Portuguese National Tourist Office (see page 177). Avid golfers should also consider the option of accommodation at a 'Golf Hotel'. Typically these are establishments very close to the top golf courses that offer free (or heavily discounted) golf on courses that may otherwise be difficult to get a game on. They also arrange golf tournaments among their guests.

Horse riding. There are stables all around the country where horses can be hired, and many *quintas* (hotels on country estates) provide horses for guests. The Algarve in particular has a number of riding centres, or *centros hípicos*. Most of the horses you'll encounter are at least part Lusitano, a famous and sure-footed Portuguese breed. Adventure centres in northern Portugal also offer horse-riding trips, such as around Campo do Gerés in the Minho.

Tennis. Major hotels tend to have their own tennis courts, but there are tennis clubs and public courts as well. Many golf clubs also have their own courts. The Algarve is home to several world-class tennis centres – one of the most impressive is at Vale do Lobo. Another famous centre is Clube de Ténis Rocha Brava near Carvoeiro. The Estoril Tennis Club is an excellent centre, too.

Walking. The many national parks in central and northern Portugal are ideal for walking and hiking: the Serra da Estrela and Peneda-Gerês and Montesinho National Parks are three of the best. The beaches and cliffs along the Algarve coast are also excellent for walking, as are the hills around Mogadouro in Trás-os-Montes.

Golf guidance

Green fees range from 40–200 euros for 18 holes. All courses are open to visitors; many require an official handicap certificate, and all require proper dress.

Campo Pequeno Praça de Touros bullring in Lisbon

SPECTATOR SPORTS

Bullfights. In Portuguese bullfights the bull is not killed in the ring, but later in a slaughterhouse. Portugal's home of bullfighting is Vila Franca de Xira (see page 53) in the Ribatejo. Fights are also staged in the Campo Pequeno Praça de Touros bullring in Lisbon (beginning in May until the end of September, with bullfights staged every Thursday and Sunday) and the Monumental arena in Cascais. Bullfights strictly organised for tourists are held at Lagos, Quarteira and Vila Real de Santo António, as well as Albufeira on the Algarve coast during the bullfighting season (look for notices advertising 'Praça de Toiros'). The season runs from Easter Sunday to October.

Football (soccer). *Futébol* always draws big crowds in Portugal. Lisbon's two major teams are Benfica and Sporting Clube de Portugal. FC Porto is the top club in Portugal's second city. The Algarve has a team in Farense, from the regional capital.

PORTUGAL FOR CHILDREN

The most popular destination for children is likely to be the beach. Most hotels have pools, many with shallow pools.

The beaches of the Algarve, with long, sandy, gently shelving beaches for small children and small rocky coves ideal for older children to explore, are perfect for family holidays. Pay attention to the beach warning flags, however. Green means the sea is calm and a lifeguard is on duty; green plus a checked flag means that no lifeguard is on duty; yellow stipulates no swimming; red means danger and warns bathers to stay ashore.

The biggest attraction in Lisbon for children is the **Parque das Nações** (see page 39) with its splendid aquarium (Oceanário de Lisboa), playgrounds, fountains, paddleboats and aerial cable cars.

Portugal dos Pequeninos (www.portugaldospequenitos. pt), in Coimbra, is a theme park of miniatures of Portugal's famous buildings.

The Algarve has a number of theme parks, zoos and waterparks, including **Aquashow** near Quarteira (between Vilamoura and Loulé; www.aquashowpark.com) at N396 Semino; **Slide & Splash** (N125 Vale de Deus, near Lagoa; www.slidesplash.com) and **Aqualand – The Big One** (N125, near Alcantarilha; www.aqualand.pt), reputedly Europe's largest. Another attraction is **Zoomarine** (N125, km 25; www.zoomarine.pt), a theme park with performing dolphins and sea lions, a parrot show, fairground rides and swimming pools. Inland, near Vaqueiros, **A Cova dos Mouros** (http://minacovamouros.sitepac.pt) is a theme park with a neolithic village built around a prehistoric copper mine – and donkey rides.

CALENDAR OF FESTIVALS AND EVENTS

February–March *Funchal, Loulé, Nazaré, Ovar, Torres Vedras*: biggest carnivals (Mardi Gras), but there are processions and fireworks everywhere. *Lisbon*: Fado Festival at various sites at carnival time.

March–April *Braga*: Pilgrimage to Bom Jesus is the largest of many Holy Week processions.

May *Barcelos*: Feast of the Crosses music concerts and a spectacular display of fireworks on the Cávado River (first weekend). *Fátima*: First pilgrimage of year to shrine (13 May). *Coimbra*: 'Queima das Fitas' (ceremonial burning of ribbons) celebration marking the end of the university's academic year.

June–July *Lisbon*: Festival of music, dance and theatre all month. Fairs and festivities for the People's Saints, honouring St Anthony (13 June), St John (24 June) and St Peter (29 June). *Vila do Conde*: Festa do Corpo de Deus procession in the old town's streets strewn with flowers. *Vila Franca de Xira*: running of bulls in the streets (first two Sundays of July).

July–August *Estoril/Cascais*: Estoril International Music Festival.

August *Guimarães*: 'Festas Gualterianas', three-day festival dating from 15th century, with religious torchlight processions, bands, folk dance groups and colourful medieval parade (4–6 August). *Viana do Castelo*: Festa da Nossa Senhora da Agonia (Our Lady of Agony Festivities), famous religious festival with traditional costumes (weekend nearest to the 20th).

September *Lamego*: festivities honouring Nossa Senhora dos Remédios, annual pilgrimage to baroque shrine, with torchlight procession, folklore festival, fairs and fireworks, ending with triumphal procession (6–9 Sept). *Nazaré*: Nossa Senhora da Nazaré (Our Lady of Nazaré): fishermen carry an image of the town's patron saint in processions; also bullfights, fairs, concerts, folk dancing *and singing (second week September)*.

October *Fátima*: last pilgrimage of year (12–13 October). *Vila Franca de Xira*: October Fair that includes bull running and bullfights (first two weeks).

November *Golegã*: National Horse Show/St Martin's Fair (second week).

December *Lisbon*: Bolsa de Natal Christmas market throughout the city.

EATING OUT

Portuguese cuisine is true to its origins, the food of fishermen and farmers. Traditional dishes are found in both expensive restaurants and the simplest of cafés. But the Portuguese can also be very inventive; you're likely to sample combinations like clams and pork, sole and bananas, or pork and figs.

Seafood fans are in luck in Portugal, with a surfeit of freshly caught fish and shellfish. The humble but noble Portuguese sardine is an inexpensive standard, especially down south, and with a hunk of local rustic bread and a bottle of house wine, you can still feast well on a small budget.

Restaurants do not skimp on meat either: you can find delicious pork and lamb dishes as well as steak. You'll also enjoy freshly picked fruit and vegetables, not to mention Portuguese wines, which are eminently drinkable.

Carne de porco à Alentejana

Some of the best dishes are regional stews – *ensopadas* of the Alentejo, *caldeiradas* of the Algarve and the *açordas* of Estremadura. These dishes are found in restaurants all over the country.

Portions in Portuguese restaurants tend to be rather large. You can also ask for a half portion *(uma meia dose)* which is usually charged at around two-thirds of the full price.

RESTAURANTS AND MENUS

Even the top restaurants are fairly affordable by the standards of European capitals. Menus displayed in the window or beside the door let you know what to expect in variety and price.

Cover charge

Nearly every restaurant in Portugal serves a *couvert* (literally, cover) – an assortment of appetisers, including bread and butter, that appear to be free but are usually not. Your bill will include a charge of a few euros for the *couvert*. Theoretically, if you don't touch them, you should not be charged for them.

Prices normally include taxes and a service charge, but it's customary to leave an additional tip of between 5 and 10 percent for good service. *Típico* restaurants specialise in local cuisine, *marisqueiras* feature seafood and *churrasqueiras* offer barbecued meat.

Many restaurants and cafés offer an *ementa turística*–tourist menu. The term does not, however, imply a poor-grade international tourist meal. Rather, it is an economically priced set meal–typically bread, butter, soup, main course and dessert. Another inexpensive option at many restaurants and cafés is the *prato do dia* (dish of the day).

Many restaurants close for the entire month of August.

MEAL TIMES

Breakfast *(pequeno almoço)* is usually eaten any time up until about 10am. Lunch *(almoço)* is served from shortly after noon until 3pm and dinner *(jantar)* runs from 7.30–10pm (or later especially in a *casa de fado*).

Snacks are usually eaten at a *pastelaria* (pastry and cake shop), *salão de chá* (tea shop), or what the Portuguese call by its English name, a 'snack bar', a stand-up counter where you can purchase sandwiches, savoury pastries and sweets.

WHAT TO EAT

Soups and starters. When you sit down to a restaurant meal you may be presented with a plate of appetisers, such as cheese or ham, that you haven't asked for. Note that any of these that you eat will have to be paid for and can be expensive, especially if it is seafood. Lunch and dinner otherwise often get off to a hearty start with soups being typical Portuguese fare. *Caldo verde* (green soup) is a traditional thick broth of potato purée with finely-shredded cabbage or kale. The best smoked ham *(presunto fumado)* comes from Chaves, the northernmost province of Portugal. Monchique ham is also highly regarded.

Seafood. The best advertisement for seafood is usually the window of a restaurant: a generous refrigerated display case with crabs and prawns, oysters and mussels, sea bass and sole. Seafood restaurants generally sell shellfish by weight, giving the price in euros per kilo. You may wish to have a calculator handy.

Fresh douradas

A number of seafood dishes are true local specialities. *Caldeirada* is a rich seafood stew. *Amêijoas na cataplana* is an invention from the Algarve of steamed mussels (or clams) with sausages, tomato, white wine, ham, onion and herbs.

> ### Preço V
>
> If you see *'preço V'* (or simply *'PV'*) beside the seafood or shellfish on a menu, it means that the price is variable depending on the day's market price. Ask the price before ordering.

Açorda de marisco is a spicy, garlic-scented thick bread-soup full of seafood bits; raw eggs are later added into the mixture. *Lulas recheadas* are squid stuffed with rice, olives, tomato, onion and herbs. Sardines *(sardinhas)* are excellent and generally served grilled *(sardinhas assadas)*. Cod *(bacalhau)* is the national dish of Portugal, even though it can be expensive and comes dried and salted, and from distant seas.

The Portuguese say that cod is served in 100, 365, or 1,000 different ways (depending on the teller's taste for hyperbole). One of the best ways to try it is in a tasty *bacalhau à Gomes de Sá*, in which flaky chunks of cod are baked with parsley, potatoes, onion and olives and garnished with grated hard-boiled egg.

Fresh fish, whole or filleted, is usually served grilled, as are outstanding *atum* (tuna) and *espadarte*, swordfish steaks. For those who know some Spanish or Portuguese, *peixe espada* might sound like swordfish; however, it is actually scabbard fish, a long, thin fish that comes from the area south of Lisbon. Swordfish is in fact *espadarte* and smoked swordfish *(espadarte fumado)* is a little like smoked salmon but with a grainier texture and less sweet.

Meat. Meat is eaten just as much as fish. *Bife na frigideira* is not what you might think. *Frigideira* means frying pan, and this dish is a beefsteak nicely done in a wine sauce. *Cabrito assado* is baked kid served with rice and potato, sometimes

Doces de ovos, one for the sweet-toothed

heavy-going but delicious. *Carne de porco à Alentejana* is an inspired dish of clams and pork cooked with paprika and garlic. *Espetada mista* is a Portuguese shish kebab: chunks of beef, lamb and pork on a spit. *Feijoada* is the national dish of Brazil, a former Portuguese colony. In Portugal, the dish is not nearly as elaborate or ritualised, but it's still a tasty stew of pigs' trotters and sausage, white beans and cabbage. Most meat dishes in Portugal are served with both rice and potatoes.

Game and fowl. *Frango* (chicken) is popular and versatile, be it stewed in wine sauce, fried, roasted, or barbecued to a tasty crisp. Some restaurants specialise in game–*codorniz* (quail), *perdiz* (partridge), *lebre* (hare) and even *javali* (wild boar).

Colonial dishes. Portugal's former colony of Goa accounts for the local popularity of *caril* (curry) and other Indian-style dishes. *Piri-piri* is a hot-pepper condiment and preparation from Angola that will set most mouths ablaze. Order a *piri-piri* dish with extreme caution.

Vegetarian dishes. Vegetarianism has made few inroads in Portugal, and there are not many restaurants dedicated to vegetarians outside the capital and the Algarve. However, vegetable soups are not hard to find and good fresh vegetables are often served as side dishes, including the popular broad beans *(favas)*. Salads are readily available. *Salada à Portuguesa* is generally made with green peppers, garlic, tomato and cucumber. Omelettes are served everywhere.

Dessert and cheese. The Portuguese sweet tooth may be a little too much for your taste. Locals pour sugar on a sliced sweet orange, after all. The cakes, custards and pastries are usually made with the basics, egg yolks and sugar, and are delicious. *Pudim flã* (also *flam*, *flan*, or *flão*) is a Portuguese caramel custard. Custard-cream tarts are a Portuguese speciality found everywhere, but the best are in Belém: *pastéis*

⊙ COZINHA PORTUGUESA

From starters to stews to sweets, Portuguese food is never bland. From the classiest city establishments to smalltown *restaurantes*, the Portuguese use herbs and spices (hot peppers only rarely) with a light touch so that flavours are enhanced but not overwhelmed. All the same, the cuisine is robust rather than subtle – and absolutely delicious. *Coentros*, coriander, is a favourite herb in *caldeiradas*, or stews, and with fish, too. Each region has its own special dishes: *rojões*, marinated pork, is popular in the Minho; *leitão assado*, roast suckling pig around Buçaco and Coimbra; *tripas*, tripe, in Porto; and clams or mussels steamed in a *cataplana* (like a closed wok) is a savoury Algarve dish. Alentejo soups might include a raw egg – and can be served to end a meal. Fish and shellfish come fresh from the sea and are sensational. *Pudins, tortas* and *pasteis*, sweet puddings, tarts and pastries, are found everywhere. Made from eggs, sugar and almonds, they are hard to resist. *Pousadas* are almost always good bets for regional cuisine.

The best Portuguese cheeses are from ewes' milk

de Belém, crisp pastry casings filled with delectable, secret-recipe cream and topped with a dusting of cinnamon. They're at their finest from the always-thronged Antigua Confeitaria de Belém, Rua de Belém 84-92, Lisbon, tel: 213 637 423, www.pasteisdebelem.pt.

Of Portuguese cheeses, the most savoury are from ewes' milk. Serra da Estrela, richest, priciest and rated the best, should be eaten when it's soft and runny. Small Azeitão cheeses from the Arribada region are full of flavour, as are cheeses made in Serpa and Nisa. Some restaurants offer small hard cheeses as an appetiser. If you prefer cheese at the end of a meal, you might try it with an *aguardente velha* (old brandy). Also on many menus is Flamengo, a mild cheese that is very similar to Edam.

Some restaurants serve *queijo fresco* as an appetizer. This is a small, white, soft mini-cheese made of ewes' and goats' milk that's beguilingly creamy.

DRINKS

Table wines. Portuguese wines are uniformly good, and several regions produce truly excellent wines. House wine *(vinho da casa)* in restaurants is generally a good bet: *tinto* is red, *rosado* pink and *branco* white.

Under EU regulations there are various categories of wine, including DOC controlled appellation wines produced in a limited geographical region. Wines from the Algarve and Alentejo are good table wines. Dão and Douro wines can be heavier.

Vinho verde from the Minho region is a light, low-alcohol, slightly sparkling young wine that goes down a treat on a sunny lunchtime.

Vinho espumante is Portuguese sparkling wine, packaged in a Champagne-shaped bottle. Most are sweetish but you can find some quite dry versions of it.

Dessert wines. The two most celebrated Portuguese wines, port and Madeira, named after their places of origin, are mostly known as dessert wines, but they may also be sipped as aperitifs. The before-dinner varieties are dry or extra dry white port and the dry Madeiras, Sercial and Verdelho.

After dinner, try one of the famous ruby or tawny ports (aged tawnys are especially good) or a Madeira dessert wine, Boal or Malvasia (Malmsey).

Other drinks. Portuguese beers are good and refreshing. Light or dark, they are served chilled, bottled, or from the tap. One of the best and most common is Sagres. You can find various brands of mineral water in small or large bottles, bubbly or still. Portuguese fruit juices can be delicious, and well-known soft drinks are also available.

Wine tasting

It's great fun to go port or wine tasting, with several fine port centres in Lisbon (see page 37) and Porto (see page 71), plus wine tours near Setúbal, close to Lisbon (see page 44). In Alentejo, there is an Alentejo Wine Route, with recommended *adegas* (wineries) you can visit; enquire at local tourist offices for details.

TO HELP YOU ORDER

We'd like a table. **Queríamos uma mesa.**
I'd like a/an/some... **Queria...**
I'd like to pay. **Queria pagar.**

beer **cerveja**
bill **a conta**
bread **pão**
butter **manteiga**
coffee **um café**
dessert **sobremesa**
fish **peixe**
fruit **fruta**
ice cream **gelado**
meat **carne**
menu **ementa**
milk **leite**

mineral water **água mineral**
napkin **guardanapo**
pepper **pimenta**
potatoes **batatas**
rice **arroz**
salad **salada**
salt **sal**
sandwich **sanduíche**
soup **sopa**
sugar **açúcar**
tea **chá**
wine **vinho**

MENU READER

alho garlic
amêijoas baby clams
atun tuna
azeitonas olives
bacalhau cod (salted)
besugo sea bream
bife (vaca) steak (beef)
bolo cake
Borrego lamb
camarões shrimp
caranguejo crab
cavala mackerel
cebola onion
chouriço spicy sausage

cogumelos mushrooms
couve cabbage
laranja orange
legumes vegetables
linguado sole
lulas squid
maçã apple
mariscos shellfish
mexilhões mussels
morangos strawberries
ostras oysters
ovo egg
porco pork
queijo cheese

PLACES TO EAT

We have used the following symbols to give an idea of the price for a three-course meal for one, including wine and service:

€€€€	over 40 euros
€€€	25–40 euros
€€	15–25 euros
€	below 15 euros

LISBON

Bico do Sapato €€€ *Avenida Infante D. Henrique (Cais da Pedra, Baixa), tel: 218 810 320, www.bicadosapato.com.* Open Tue–Sat for lunch and dinner, Sun 12.30–4pm, Mon dinner only. Part-owned by John Malkovich. Trendy restaurant across from Santa Apolónia station. Excellent and fairly priced creative cuisine, good local wines. Sushi bar on the first floor (dinner only). Closed Jul–Aug.

Cervejeria da Trindade €€ *Rua Nova da Trindade 20 (Bairro Alto), tel: 213 423 506.* Open daily for lunch and dinner (until late). A famous old beer hall and restaurant in a former monastery. Popular Portuguese cooking and seafood specialities at good prices.

Chapitô á Mesa €€–€€€ *Costa do Castelo 7, tel: 218 875 077,* http://chapito.org. Open daily for lunch and dinner (until late). Amazing views across Lisbon – ask for a terrace table with a view. The food is hearty and tasty, with a barbecue downstairs and posher fare in the restaurant.

Frade dos Mares €€€ *Avenida dom Carlos 1, 55-A, tel: 213 909 418, www.fradedosmares.com.* Open daily lunch and dinner. This smart, albeit a little bit dark, restaurant is famous among locals and tourists for its great seafood and meat dishes.

Gambrinus €€€€ *Rua das Portas de Santo Antão 23 (Baixa), tel: 213 421 466, www.gambrinuslisboa.com.* Open daily for lunch and dinner (until late). Sophisticated, wood-panelled restaurant near Rossio. Specialises in traditional Portuguese and Galician dishes, which means fresh seafood.

Pap d'Açorda €€€€ *Rua da Atalaia 57 (Bairro Alto)*, tel: 213 464 811, https://papacorda.com. Open Sun, Tue, Wed noon–midnight, Thu–Sat noon–2am. One of Lisbon's hippest spots to eat, cool and informal. Traditional and creative Portuguese dishes such as the restaurant's namesake *açorda de marisco* (a delicious, thick shellfish stew with lobster and shrimp).

Tavares €€€€ *Rua da Misericórdia 37 (Bairro Alto)*, tel: 213 421 112, www.restaurantetavares.net. Open Mon–Sat for dinner. A stylish and immensely popular restaurant-café with ornate ceilings, mirrors and chandeliers. Serving classical French cuisine for two centuries.

NEAR LISBON

Cozinha Velha €€€ *Palácio Nacional de Queluz, Largo do Palácio, Queluz*, tel: 214 356 158, www.pousadas.pt. Open daily for lunch and dinner. Atmospheric restaurant in former kitchen of the royal palace. Excellent regional cooking. Specialities include stewed partridge with chestnuts and grapes, and goat's cheese with walnuts and honey wrapped in pastry.

ESTREMADURA AND RIBATEJO

Bela Vista €€ *Rua da Fonte do Choupo 6, Tomar*, tel: 249 312 870, http://restaurantebelavista.pai.pt/. Open daily for lunch and dinner. Old house with great views of historic Tomar from across the river. Try the *frango à caril* (curried chicken).

O Sabor da Pedra €€€ *Rua do Rio 5, Alverangel, São Pedro deTomar, Tomar*, tel: 249 371 750, www.osabordapedra.com. Open daily for lunch and dinner. A traditional restaurant offering splendid views of the lake and good Portuguese food. Its speciality is *cabrito assado* (baked kid).

Pousada de Óbidos €€€ *Paço Real, Óbidos, tel: 210 407 630.* Open daily for lunch and dinner. Delightful restaurant within an historic Óbidos *pousada* occupying a medieval castle. Good regional cooking, including specialities such as royal duck and crab pie.

Restaurante Tia Alice €€€€ *Rua do Adro, Fátima, tel: 249 531 737.* Closed Sun night, Mon and all of July. Charming, rustic eatery in an old house. *Açorda* (egg and vegetable dish), goat stew and cod with béchamel sauce are the signature dishes.

THE BEIRAS

Adega Paço do Conde € *Rua Paço do Conde 1, Coimbra, tel: 239 825 605.* Open Mon–Sat for lunch and dinner. In the commercial area of the old town, an extremely popular bargain restaurant for grilled meats and fish. Always packed.

Arcadas da Cappella €€€€ *António Augusto Gonçalves, Coimbra, tel: 239 802 380,* www.quintadaslagrimas.pt. Open daily for lunch and dinner. Superb continental restaurant in Quinta das Lágrimas hotel with great Portuguese specialities created by chef Albano Lourenço; extensive wine list.

Bussaco Palace Hotel €€–€€€€ *Mata do Bussaco, tel: 231 937 970,* www. almeidahotels.pt/pt/hotel-coimbra-portugal. Open daily for lunch and dinner. Elegant restaurant in spectacular setting of a legendary royal palace (and today hotel). *Prix-fixe* menus are good but can't compete with the dining room.

Cortiço €€ *Rua Augusto Hilário 45, Viseu, tel: 232 416 127.* Open daily for lunch and dinner. Atmospheric traditional restaurant in the historic centre, with dining rooms on both sides of the street. Regional cuisine and home cooking, heavy on meat and game.

PORTO AND THE DOURO VALLEY

Cufra €€ *Avenida da Boavista 2504, Porto, tel: 226 172 715,* www.cufra. pt. Open daily for lunch and dinner. The best place to try *francesinha*, traditional sandwich from Porto made with cold meats, melted cheese and spicy sauce made of tomato and beer.

D' Tonho €€€ *Cais da Ribeira 13-15, Porto, tel: 222 085 791/222 004 307,* www.dtonho.com. Open daily for lunch and dinner. Beautifully positioned old townhouse on the riverfront. Owned by Rui Velosa, a Portuguese pop star. The speciality is Portuguese cod casserole. Chic but relaxed. Good wine list. Booking essential.

O Comercial €€€ *Palácio da Bolsa, Rua Ferreira Borges, Porto, tel: 918 838 649,* www.ocomercial.com. Open Mon–Fri for lunch and dinner, Sat for dinner. Spectacular restaurant with a formal, time-warp atmosphere, a roaring fire in winter and tasty traditional Portuguese fare.

Rabelo (Vintage House) €€€–€€€€ *Rua António Manuel Saraiva, 5085 Pinhão, tel: 220 133 137.* Open daily for lunch and dinner. Elegant award-winning restaurant in beautiful hotel: dining room has vaulted ceilings and murals. Portuguese specialities such as *sopa de tomate à Portuguesa* (tomato soup with poached egg and bread), grilled fish and meats (veal with port wine and mushrooms). Great library bar to retire to for a glass of port.

MINHO

Bagoeira €€ *Avenida Sidónio Pais 495, Barcelos, tel: 253 813 088,* www. bagoeira.com. Open daily for lunch and dinner. Popular local place with 19th-century decor; packed on market days. Authentic regional fare such as grilled meats and local sweets, like stuffed oranges.

O Hool €€€ *Rua de Santa Maria, Largo da Oliveira, Guimarães, tel: 253 519 390,* www.hoteldaoliveira.com. Open daily for lunch and dinner. In central Guimarães, this charming *pousada* offers very good Portuguese and international cuisine in the dining room, which has wooden beams, leather chairs and exposed stone. Try the *bife especial à pousada* (châteaubriand).

Pousada do Gêres, Santa Maria do Bouro €€€ *Amares, tel: 210 407 650,* www.pousadas.pt. Open daily for lunch and dinner. Stunning, cavernous dining hall with a modern simplicity, in a former Cistercian monastery (see page 185). Great bar area with giant fireplace. Local dishes like pork loin stew, codfish with cornbread and cabbage, topped off by a massive dessert buffet of regional sweets.

TRÁS-OS-MONTES

Cozinha do Convento (Forte de São Francisco) €€€ *Chaves, tel: 276 333 700,* www.fortesaofrancisco.com. Open daily for lunch and dinner. Elegant restaurant in hotel carved out of a 16th-century convent, overlooking a large pool. Focuses on reasonably priced regional mountain cuisine. Wines are brought up from the extensive cellar in the old cistern. Separate, atmospheric tavern for informal meals.

Restaurante Carvalho €€€ *Alameda de Tabolado, Largo das Caldas 4 Chaves, tel: 276 321 727.* Open daily except Sunday dinner and Mondays. This parkside restaurant is one of Chaves' finest and offers delicious takes on regional dishes.

Solar do Bragançano €€ *Praça da Sé, 34, Bragança, tel: 273 323 875.* Open daily for lunch and dinner. Excellent restaurant occupying three rooms on the first floor of an old noble house on the main square. Elegant but laid back, with rustic furnishings, chandeliers and fresh flowers everywhere. Exotic meats, game and an excellent-value five-course *menu turístico* are the main attractions.

ALENTEJO

Cozinha de Santo Humberto €€ *Rua da Moeda 39, Évora, tel: 266 701 874.* Open Tue–Sun for lunch and dinner. On a small street off Praça Giraldo, this highly recommended restaurant is situated in an ancient cellar loaded with antiques of all sorts. Serves classic dishes of the Alentejo region and is particularly strong on game dishes like wild boar and partridge.

O Ermita €€€€ *Aldeia da Serra, Redondo, tel: 266 989 160,* www.hotel conventosaopaulo.com. Open daily for lunch and dinner. Set in an isolated 12th-century convent (Hotel Convento de São Paulo, see page 186), this is an exquisite restaurant with vaulted ceilings, 18th-century frescoes and beautiful *azulejos*. The place to go for a special occasion. Delicious Alentejo specialities.

Pousada de Évora Restaurant €€€ *Largo Conde de Vila Flor, Évora, tel: 266 730 070*. Open daily for lunch and dinner. Beautiful dining room in the cloister of an old convent (see page 98 and 186), now a sought-after *pousada*. Serves a varied selection of regional Alentejano cuisine, such as codfish with coriander and fish soup with mint.

São Rosas €€–€€€ *Largo D. Dinis 11, Estremoz, tel: 268 333 345*. Open Tue–Sun for lunch and dinner. An elegant but understated restaurant next to the castle *pousada* with beamed ceilings and earthy furnishings. Local dishes include grilled scabbard fish and roast pork loin with apple sauce. Good-value 'tourist menu' for both lunch and dinner.

THE ALGARVE

A Quinta €€€ *Rua Vale Formoso Almancil, tel: 289 393 357,* www.aquinta restaurant.com. Open Mon–Sat for dinner. An old farmhouse on the road to Loulé from Almancil and the N125 with views to the sea. Popular with the business lunch crowd so it's best to book. Lots of fish on a broad menu.

Casa Velha €€€€ *Quinta do Lago (Almancil), tel: 289 394 983/289 390 700,* www.quintadolago.com. Open Tue–Sat for dinner. Chic restaurant in a renovated 19th-century farmhouse; about as elegant as dining in the Algarve gets. French menu and excellent wine cellar.

Marisqueira Rui €€€ *Rua Comendador Vilarinho 27, Silves, tel: 282 442 682,* www.marisqueirarui.pt. Closed Tue, rest of the week lunch and dinner. An almost total concentration on succulent seafood served to an enthusiastic clientele. Cheerful rather than smart and loud with cracking shells.

Monte da Eira €€€ *Clareanes, on road from Loulé to Querença, tel: 289 438 129,* www.restaurantemontedaeira.com. Open Tue–Sat for lunch and dinner, for lunch on Sun. Away from the hordes, a skilled chef has made a modest farmhouse one of the Algarve's most successful restaurants. Portuguese food with flavour and imagination.

Quatro Águas €€€ *Estrada das 4 Águas 19 (Tavira), tel: 281 381 271*. Open daily for lunch and dinner. Handsome 18th-century building on the harbour. Traditional Portuguese dining, with an emphasis on seafood dishes like *arroz de marisco* (seafood rice) and octopus stew.

Rei das Praias €€€ *between Ferragudo and Carvoeiro, tel: 282 461 006*, www.restaurantereidaspraias.com. Open daily all day from 9am. Beautifully situated on the Caneiros beach, a good quality restaurant serving excellent food – seafood especially – and an excellent selection of wines. Booking is advisable.

Restaurante do Hotel Villa Joya €€€€ *in Hotel Villa Joya, Praia de Galé, tel: 289 591 795*, www.vilajoya.com. Open daily for lunch and dinner, although closing day may vary. Refined two-Michelin stars hotel restaurant, with wonderful sea views, preparing eclectic international dishes. Booking is essential.

Vivendo €€€ *Rua Ruy Belo,* Estrada Da Meia Praia, *Lagos, tel: 282 770 902*, www.vila-palmeira.com. Open Tue–Sun for lunch and dinner. Friendly chef Christoph Voigt greets his guests personally. Food is great, especially the melon and ham starter and tiramisu for dessert. Booking is essential.

A-Z TRAVEL TIPS

A SUMMARY OF PRACTICAL INFORMATION

A

ACCOMMODATION

Hotels are graded from 2-star to 5-star deluxe. Rates are lower in less elaborate hostelries: an *estalagem* or inn; a *pensão* (rooms with meals available); or *residencial* (rooms, generally without meals). In Lisbon, you can also rent serviced apartments, while in the countryside, rustic stays in former manor houses are common.

Pousadas are national inns, usually in historic buildings, such as monasteries, castles and convents, and at scenic sites. For more information, visit the website www.pousadas.pt; various promotions are offered whereby you can get reduced rates, including for honeymooners and for over-55s.

Turihab and **Solares de Portugal** are government schemes: private properties adapted or totally converted for use by guests (tel: 258 931 750; www.solaresdeportugal.pt or www.turihab.pt, tel: 258 741 672). They are in three groups: Casas Antigas are manor houses from the 17th and 18th centuries; Quintas e Herdades are country estates and farms including the wine estates of the north; Casas Rústicas are cottages and rustic houses in typical regional style.

You may want to rent a villa or apartment for your stay. If so, try websites such as Owners Direct (www.ownersdirect.co.uk), Portugal Villa (www.portugalvilla.com), or Popular Villas (www.popularvillas.com).

It's best to book a couple of months ahead in high season (mid-June to mid-September). Some hotels close over low season; others often offer discounts, especially in the coastal resorts.

I'd like a single/double room with a bath/shower **Queria um quarto simples/duplo com banho/chuveiro**
What is the rate per night? **Qual é o preço por noite?**

AIRPORTS

Portugal has three international airports: Lisbon, Faro and Porto.

Lisbon Airport is only 7km (4 miles) from the city centre, a 15-minute drive (allow twice as long at rush hour). Besides taxis, which are plentiful and charge about €10-15 to the centre of Lisbon, you can take several busses (lines 208, 705, 722,744, 783), the airport shuttle (Aerobus; www. aerobus.pt), which leaves about every 20 minutes from 7.30am–11pm. They pass through the city centre, including the Rossio, on the way to Cais do Sodré train station. However, the quickest and most convenient way to get to the city centre is on the Metro (red line, 6.30am–1am), which takes you to the downtown in 20 minutes. For airport information: tel: 218 413 500.

Faro International Airport, serving the Algarve, is 4km (2.5 miles) from Faro, the regional capital. It's a 10-minute taxi ride (around €10) to Faro and about half an hour by car to Albufeira. There's also a bus service (lines 14 and 16; www.proximo.pt) to Faro. For airport information: tel: 289 800 800.

Porto's Francisco Sá Carneiro airport lies about 20 minutes north of the town, towards Matosinhos. It's a 45-minute journey on the metro Line E (Violet) line. You can also take an STCP bus (www.stcp.pt) or taxi for around €20–30, but it can take around an hour in heavy traffic. For airport information, tel: 229 432 400.

TAP Air Portugal (www.tapportugal.com) information is tel: 707 205 700. The website for all of Portugal's major airports is www.ana.pt.

> Where do I get the bus to the airport? **Onde posso apanhar o autocarro para o aeroporto?**
> centre of the city **centro da cidade**

B

BUDGETING FOR YOUR TRIP

Portugal is generally cheaper than many European destinations. However, the exchange rate and the season will affect the cost of your trip.

Transport to Portugal. For Europeans, Lisbon, Faro and Porto are a short, direct flight away, usually 2–3 hours. Regularly scheduled flights may not be inexpensive, but you are likely to find a fair choice of discounts and charter flights, especially from London. For those travelling from beyond Europe, the flight will be a considerably greater expenditure, though you may also be able to find packages and specials. Scheduled flights from England and continental Europe may cost anywhere from £100–300 return. Package deals including airline and hotel can be economical.

Sights. Around €2.50–12, depending on the nature of the exhibit.

Accommodation. Hotels at the top levels are comparable to those in large European cities but differ greatly according to season. July to August in the Algarve, hotel prices are exorbitant – often double off-season rates. In high season, a double room with bath per night in a 3-star hotel averages €75–100; 4-star hotel, €125–200; 5-star hotel, €200–400. *Pousadas* are generally €120–280 for a double room depending on the style of the building. Bear in mind that most do not include breakfast. City tax is charged in Lisbon (€1 per person per night for up to seven consecutive days) and Porto (€2 per person per night).There is also a 6 percent IVA (value added) tax.

Meals. Even top-rated restaurants may be surprisingly affordable compared to most European cities. Portuguese wines are usually good and very attractively priced, even in fine restaurants. A three-course meal with wine in a reasonable establishment averages about €15–30 per person. The midday meal bargain, the *ementa turística*, is often no more than €20 for a fixed price three-course meal.

Drinks. Non-alcoholic drinks cost around €1–3; alcoholic beverages anything from €3–13. It's all about where you're drinking.

Local transport. Buses and taxis are reasonably priced. Local buses are about €1.50; a taxi costs between €4 and €10 for most fares within a resort or town.

Nightlife and entertainment. Costs vary widely. Expect cover fees at clubs to range from €10–20 (usually includes first drink); casino entrance, €10 or free.

C

CAMPING

Camping is very popular in Portugal, and there are sites all over the country. Buy the Roteiro Campista (www.roteiro-campista.pt; about €8), which lists most Portuguese campsites, online or at local bookshops and tourist offices. The best sites are run by Orbitur (www.orbitur.pt). Information on camping can also be obtained from tourist offices (see page 176) or the Federação de Campismo e Montanhismo de Portugal, Avenida Coronel Eduardo Galhardo 24 D; tel: 218 126 890; www.fcmportugal.com. You can also pay a visit to www.campingportugal.org which lists campsites in Portugal.

You can only camp at recognised sites. Some natural parks require camping permits and some sites require membership of an international camping organisation. You will also have to produce a passport.

Is there a campsite near here? **Há algun parque de campismo por aqui perto?**
May we camp here? **Podemos acampar aqui?**
We have a caravan (trailer). **Temos uma caravana.**

CAR HIRE

International and local firms operate in major cities and the major tourist areas. The minimum age for renting a car is 21–25 (depending on the company), and you must have a valid licence held for at least one year. Most rental companies will accept your home country's national driving licence.

Economy-class car hire is cheaper than in most parts of Europe; expect to pay €30–60 per day (including collision insurance and requisite taxes). You may find even better bargains at local firms. Rates are usually lower if contracted and paid for in advance in your home country. Find out what insurance is included.

A value-added tax (IVA; 6 percent on most products and services) is added to the total charge, but will have been included if you have paid before arrival. Third-party insurance is required and included, but full collision coverage is advisable as well. Many credit cards automatically include this if you use the card to pay for the car, but be sure to verify this before departure. Renting at an airport may incur a surcharge.

Good local firms include Portugal Auto Rentals (tel: 236 218 999; www.portugal-auto-rentals.com), while international companies include Europcar (tel: 21 940 77 90; www.europcar.pt), Avis (tel: 21 754 78 21; www.avis.com.pt), Holiday Autos (tel: +351 308 800 771; www.holiday autos.com), and Hertz (tel: 21 9426385; www.hertz.com.pt). There are plenty of hire offices at the major airports.

> I'd like to rent a car today/tomorrow for one day/a week
> **Queria alugar um carro para hoje/amanhã por um dia/ uma semana**
> Please include full insurance. **Todos os riscos, por favor.**

CLIMATE

Portugal's climate is kind, especially in the exceptionally sunny Algarve, where summers are warm and winters mild. Lisbon and the Alentejo, especially, can be uncomfortably hot in summer. (Always carry a bottle of water.) Further north the weather can be cold in winter, especially in the mountains. Average air temperatures are:

		Jan	Mar	May	July	Sept	Nov
Lisbon	°C/°F	11/52	14/57	17/63	22/72	22/72	14/57
Faro	°C/°F	12/54	13/55	18/65	24/75	22/72	16/61
Bragança	°C/°F	4/39	8/47	13/55	21/70	17/63	8/46

CLOTHING

The Algarve has a Mediterranean climate – outside high summer you might need something warmer for the evenings. Further north, warmer clothes may be necessary, especially if you are going inland or to mountainous regions. Be prepared for rain. Most restaurants are informal, but bring something smart to eat out at the grander establishments.

CRIME AND SAFETY

Portugal in general is a safe country although you should take the usual precautions. Major tourist areas such as the Algarve experience more petty crime than other parts of Portugal, though crimes involving violence against tourists are rare. Theft from rental cars is the most common crime. In rural areas the problem is far less acute, but in resorts and where cars are left unattended for a period of time the risk is high. Burglaries of holiday apartments, though less common than car theft, also occur, so be on your guard. Take the same precautions as you would at home.

Report any theft to the hotel receptionist, the nearest police station or the local tourist office. You must report any losses to the local police within 24 hours and obtain a copy of your statement for insurance purposes. If you need help, call 112.

Lisbon is infamous for its pickpockets, particularly on the Metrò and Rossio square. They operate on buses and historic trams frequented by tourists. You are also advised to take special care in the Bairro Alto or Alfama areas at night.

I want to report a theft. **Quero denunciar um roubo.**

D

DISABLED TRAVELLERS

Portugal is gradually catering more to travellers with disabilities and there is a handful of organisations that may be able to advise you further. Accessible Portugal (Rua Jorge Barradas, 50–4 F, Lisbon, tel: 926 910 989, www.accessibleportugal.com) offers a wide choice of itineraries, including city breaks, overnight trips, accommodation and tours. They speak English. Newer and larger hotels generally have disabled-accessible rooms and adapted toilets, and museums and major sights are gradually providing ramped access.

DRIVING

If you take your own car, you'll need your national driving licence, registration papers and insurance–third-party coverage is obligatory.

Road conditions. The rules of the road are the same as in most western European countries. The vehicle on the roundabout has priority unless road markings or lights indicate otherwise. Seat belts are compulsory and you are subject to a stiff fine if caught without one. Local driving standards can be erratic. In towns, pedestrians nominally have priority at crossings – but if you're walking, don't count on it.

Speed limits are 120kph (75mph) on motorways, 100km (62mph) on roads restricted to motor vehicles, 90kph (56mph) on other roads and 50kph (37mph) in urban areas. Minimum speeds are posted (in blue) for some motorway lanes and suspension bridges. Cars towing caravans (trailers) are restricted to 50kph (31mph) in towns and 70kph (45mph) on the open road and motorways. Most motorways have tolls *(portagem)*. Many Portuguese disregard speed limits, but that doesn't mean you should.

Fuel costs. Fuel by the litre (about €1.44 at the time of writing) is expensive in Portugal. Prices, controlled by the government, should be almost the same everywhere you go. Many petrol stations are open 24 hours, and all accept credit cards.

Parking. You have to park facing the same direction as the flow of traffic on that side of the road. Unless there's an indication to the contrary, you can park for as long as you wish. Certain areas are metered and others are 'Blue Zones', where you must buy a ticket from a machine. Parking lots and garages are also available.

If you need help. If your automobile organisation is affiliated with the Automóvel Clube de Portugal (Rua Rosa Araújo 24, Lisbon; tel: 219 429 113; 24h assistance: 808 222 222; www.acp.pt), you can use their services free of charge. Otherwise, most garages in Portugal can handle the usual problems.

Road signs. Standard international pictograms are used in Portugal, but you might also encounter the following signs:

crossroads **cruzamento**
danger **perigo**
detour (diversion) **desvio**
keep right/left **seguir pela direita/esquerda**
no entry **passagem proíbida**
no parking **estacionamento proíbido**
no through road **sem saída**
no through traffic **trânsito proíbido**
one-way street **sentido único**
pedestrians **pedestres/peões**
stop **alto/pare/stop**
slow down **afrouxe/reduza**
steep hill **descida ingreme**
roadworks (men working)/end of roadworks **obras/fim de
    obras**
Are we on the right road for...? **É esta a estrada para...?**
Fill the tank with super, please. **Encha o depósito de
    super, por favor.**
Check the oil/tires/battery, please. **Verifique o óleo/os
    pneus/a bateria, se faz favor.**
I've broken down. **O meu carro está avariado.**
There's been an accident. **Houve um acidente.**

E

ELECTRICITY

Portugal is 220-volt, 50-cycle AC. Sockets comply with European standards. An adaptor (UK, US) and a transformer (US) is needed for American and British appliances.

> I need an adaptor/a battery, please. **Preciso de um adaptador/uma pilha, por favor**.

EMBASSIES AND CONSULATES

Embassies are listed in local phone books (under *Consulado* or *Embaixada*). Most are in Lisbon, Porto or Faro.

Embassies in Lisbon

Australia Avenida da Liberdade 200, tel: 213 101 500; http://portugal.embassy.gov.au/.

Canada (Embassy/Consulate): Avenida da Liberdade 198-200, Edifico Victoria; tel: 213 164 600; www.canadainternational.gc.ca/portugal.

Republic of Ireland (Embassy/Consulate): Avenida da Liberdade No 200, 4th Floor; tel: 213 308 200; www.dfa.ie/irish-embassy/portugal/.

South Africa (Embassy): Avenida Luís Bivar 10/10 A; tel: 213 192 200; www.embaixada-africadosul.pt.

UK (Embassy): Rua de São Bernardo 33; tel: 213 924 000; www.gov.uk/world/organisations/british-embassy-lisbon.

US (Embassy/Consulate): Avenida das Forças Armadas 1600; tel: 217 273 300; https://pt.usembassy.gov/.

Consulates in the Algarve

Some European countries have consuls in the Algarve.

British Consulate (Consulado da Grã Bretanha), handles Commonwealth nationals: Avenida Guanaré, 8501-915 Portimão; tel: 282 490 750.

Canadian Consulate (Consulado de Canadá): Rua Frei Lourenço de Sta

Maria 1, 8001 Faro; tel: 289 803 757.

Most embassies and consulates are open Mon–Fri 9 or 10am–5pm, with a break in the middle of the day of 1–2.5 hours.

EMERGENCIES

For all emergencies, tel: 112. Although you can call the police from any one of the blue boxes in the street marked *polícia*, it's unlikely anyone on the other end will speak anything but Portuguese.

ETIQUETTE

The Portuguese are usually courteous and hospitable. Taking a shot while to learn and use the language basics will serve you well. There are always orderly queues at bus stops; be certain to respect them. If you are invited to someone's house, it is polite to bring flowers for the hostess. Stretching in public is considered rude. Otherwise, use common sense and a smile and you shouldn't go far wrong.

G

GETTING TO PORTUGAL

Air travel. Lisbon's and Porto's airports are linked by regularly scheduled daily non-stop flights from several European cities. There are also direct flights to Lisbon from the US and Canada. From Lisbon a flight connection can be made to Faro in the Algarve.

Regularly scheduled, low cost and cheap charter flights to Lisbon, Porto and Faro (mostly in summer) are available from the UK, Ireland and most major cities in Western Europe. Scheduled flights by TAP Air Portugal and British Airways are usually more expensive, although they usually offer special deals outside of the high season. Booking ahead is always wise.

The national Portuguese airline is **TAP/Air Portugal** (tel: 707 205 700 anywhere in Portugal; Lisbon, tel: 707 205 700 or 218 415 000; London, tel: 0345 601 0932; www.flytap.com).

By car. Many people coming for long stays in Portugal take their cars from other points in Europe by major motorways through Spain and Portugal. British travellers can take their cars across the Channel to France or Spain and make the drive from there, although a relaxed trip would be likely to take three or four days.

The main access road to Lisbon and the Algarve from France, through Spain, is at the western end of the Pyrenees. A motorway (expressway) runs from Biarritz (France) to Burgos. From there, take the N1 to Madrid and continue on the E4 via Badajoz and Setúbal, or the E4 to Mérida and then go via the E102 through Seville. The distance from Calais to the Algarve is over 2,000km (1,300 miles); you might consider the long-distance car ferry service from Plymouth to Santander in northern Spain (a 24-hour trip). From Santander, follow the N611 to the E3 via Valladolid and Coimbra.

By rail. Portugal is linked to the European railway network; connections to Lisbon are possible from points throughout Spain, France and the rest of continental Europe.

The Portuguese national railway network is called **CP** (Comboios de Portugal, tel: 707 210 220; www.cp.pt). The Santa Apolónia station in Lisbon (Avenida Dom Henrique 73) or the Oriente station in Parque des Nações serve all international trains. Daily international trains run between Paris and Lisbon (Sud Express), crossing the frontier at Vilar Formoso; between Lisbon and Madrid, crossing the frontier at Marvão; and between Porto and Vigo, crossing the frontier at Valença. Connecting trains to the Algarve depart from Lisbon's Santa Apolónia or Oriente stations, crossing the River Tegus (Tejo) on the 25 de Abril bridge (Ponte do Tejo).

Europeans travelling to and within Portugal by train can opt to buy an InterRail Pass (www.interrail.eu): the InterRail Global Pass allows travel within 30 European countries, including Portugal, five out of 15 continuous days or five, seven, 10 or 15 days within one continuous month; the InterRail One Country Pass allows three, four, six or eight days' travel within Portugal during one month. Non-Europeans can buy a Eurail Pass (www.eurail.com): the Eurail Global Pass allows travel within 28 European countries, including Portugal, from 5 days to three months; the Eurail One Country Pass allows 3–8 days' travel within Portugal within two months.

By sea. Lisbon is a major port, and several cruise ships include a port-of-call in the capital. Ferries from Great Britain go to Santander, Spain, from Plymouth and Portsmouth, and to Bilbao, Spain, from Portsmouth. Crossings range from 24 to 36 hours. The drive from northern Spain to the Algarve is then likely to take another 15 to 18 hours.

GUIDES AND TOURS

Information on any variety of sightseeing tours is available from tourist information offices (see page 176), travel agents and hotels.

All the excursion firms, such as **Cityrama** (tel: 213 191 070; www.cityrama.pt), offer trips to Mafra, Queluz, Sintra, Cascais and Estoril, as well as a long day's outing to the major sites north of Lisbon, which include Fátima, Alcobaça and Batalha, Óbidos and Nazaré.

Between June and October, Comboios de Portugal (www.cp.pt), the state railway company, run a trip on an historic steam train along the banks of the river Douro from Régua to Tua.

If you are travelling independently, you can cover all these at greater leisure, perhaps making an overnight stop or two on the way. Another company that organises tours for single people, families or groups is Tours for You (tel: 213 904 208; www.toursforyou.pt).

> We'd like an English-speaking guide **Queremos um guia que fale inglês**.

H

HEALTH AND MEDICAL CARE

Standards of hygiene are generally very high; the most likely illness to befall travellers will be due to an excess of sun or alcohol. The water is safe to drink, but bottled water is cheaply available everywhere and most locals drink it too.

Farmácias (drugstores/chemists) are open during normal business hours. At other times one shop in each neighbourhood is on duty around the clock. Addresses are listed in newspapers.

For more serious illness or injury, the **British Hospital** (Rua Tomas da Fronseca Edifico BeF, Torres da Lisboa, Lisbon; tel: 217 194 600; www.british-hospital.pt) and the British Hospital Saldanha-Mirocular on Av. Praia da Vitória, n 71 – 2 B (tel: 217 104 600) have English-speaking staff.

Medical insurance to cover illness or accident while abroad is a good investment. EU nationals with the European Health Insurance Card (EHIC) obtained well before departure get free emergency treatment at Social Security and Municipal hospitals in Portugal. Privately billed hospital visits are expensive.

Where's the nearest pharmacy? **Onde fica a farmácia mais perto?**
I need a doctor/dentist. **Preciso de um médico/dentista.**
Get a doctor quickly. **Chame um médico, depressa.**
an ambulance **uma ambulância**
hospital **hospital**
an upset stomach **mal do estômago**
sunstroke **uma insolação**
fever **febre**

L

LANGUAGE

Portuguese, a derivative of Latin, is spoken in such far-flung spots as Brazil, Angola, Mozambique, Timor, São Tomé and Principe, Cabo Verde and Macau – former colonies of Portugal. High-school Spanish may help with signs and menus, but will not unlock the mysteries of spoken Portuguese. The Portuguese in Portugal is much more closed and guttural-sounding, and is also spoken much faster than in Brazil.

Almost everyone understands Spanish and many speak French. A surprising number of people in Lisbon, the Algarve and elsewhere speak passable if not wholly fluent English. Schoolchildren are taught French and English, as well as Portuguese.

The *Berlitz Portuguese Phrasebook & Dictionary* covers most situations you're likely to encounter during a visit to Portugal.

good evening **boa noite**
goodbye **adeus**
excuse me/you're welcome **perdão/de nada**
please/thank you **faz favor/obrigado**
where/when/how **onde/quando/como**
yesterday/today/tomorrow **ontem/hoje/amanhã**
day/week/month/year **dia/semana/mês/ano**
left/right **esquerdo/direito**
good/bad **bom/mau**
big/small **grande/pequeno**
cheap/expensive **barato/caro**
hot/cold **quente/frio**
old/new **velho/novo**
open/closed **aberto/fechado**
Please write it down. **Escreva-lo, por favor.**
What does this mean? **O Que quer dizer isto?**
Help me, please. **Ajude-me, por favor.**
Just a minute. **Um momento.**
here/there **aqui/ali**
free (vacant)/occupied **livre/ocupado**
early/late **cedo/tarde**
easy/difficult **fácil/difícil**
Is there an admission charge? **Paga-se entrada?**

LGBTQ TRAVELLERS

In a country heavily influenced by the Catholic Church, attitudes towards gays are not as tolerant as elsewhere in Europe. Lisbon is the most important city in Portugal's gay scene and offers a number of bars and clubs catering to a gay crowd. In certain enclaves of the Algarve, such as 'the Strip' in Albufeira, gay visitors will find accommodating bars and restaurants. The website, www.portugalgay.pt, contains a travel guide for gays and lesbians, with information in English and other languages. Lisbon celebrates the annual Gay Pride Festival every June with a march down Avenida da Liberdade and celebrations throughout the city.

M

MAPS

The tourist information offices in most towns are well-stocked with maps sufficient for most purposes, including maps of transport networks. The red, green and yellow 'Portugal Touristic Map' available at some tourist information offices covers the entire country.

MEDIA

Europe's principal newspapers, including most British dailies and the *International Herald Tribune*, edited in Paris, are available on the day of publication at many newsstands and hotels. The most important Portuguese-language dailies are *Correio da Manhã* and *Diário de Notícias*.

Several television channels, including the oldest RTP1 and RTP2 run by RTP public broadcaster, are widely available in Portugal. Films are usually shown in the original language with subtitles. Most hotels at the 3-star level and above have satellite TV.

Do you have any English-language newspapers? **Tem jornais em inglês?**

MONEY

Currency (*moeda*). In common with most other European countries, the euro (€) is the official currency used in Portugal. Notes are denominated in 5, 10, 20, 50, 100, 200 and 500 euros; coins in 1 and 2 euros and 1, 2, 5, 10, 20 and 50 cents.

Currency exchange (*banco; câmbio*). Normal banking hours are Mon–Fri 8.30am–3pm. In tourist areas, some banks remain open later and at weekends to change money, and there are 24-hour exchange offices at the airports. Private exchange booths operate in all major cities.

> Can I pay with this credit card? **Posso pagar com cartão de crédito?**
> I want to change some pounds/dollars. **Queria trocar libras/dólares.**
> Can you cash a traveller's cheque? **Pode pagar um cheque de viagem?**

A substantial flat rate fee is charged for changing traveller's cheques; you have to show your passport. ATMs are much the easiest method of obtaining euros and they provide by far the best exchange rates.

Credit cards (*cartão de crédito*). These may not be accepted in some shops and restaurants, especially in small towns outside Lisbon.

Traveller's cheques. These can be cashed at any bank.

O

OPENING TIMES

Most shops and offices are open 9 or 10am–7pm weekdays (some close for lunch from 1–3pm), and 9am–1pm Saturday. Most museums are closed on Mondays and public holidays; palaces' opening hours vary and should be checked ahead. On every other day (including Sunday) they are open 10 or 11am–5pm, but most close from noon–2pm or 1–2.30pm. Some shopping malls in the larger cities open 10am–11pm or midnight, including Sunday.

Sunday **domingo**
Monday **segunda-feira**
Tuesday **terça-feira**
Wednesday **quarta-feira**
Thursday **quinta-feira**
Friday **sexta-feira**
Saturday **sábado**
Are you open tomorrow? **Estão abertos amanhã?**
When do you close? **Quándo estão fechados?**

P

POLICE

Police with armbands marked CD (*Corpo Distrital*, or local corps) are assigned to assist tourists and can usually speak a little English. Traffic is controlled by the Guarda Nacional Republicana (GNR) in white cars or on motorcycles. For a general emergency, tel: 112.

Where's the nearest police station? **Onde fica o posto de polícia mais próximo?**

POST OFFICES

Post offices are indicated by the letters CTT (Correios, Telegrafos e Telefones; www.ctt.pt). The mail service is generally good, though it can be slow in peak season. You can buy stamps from most shops as well – they usually display a sign that says *Correios*. Most post boxes are red.

Main offices are generally open 9am–6pm Monday–Friday. Main post offices in the major cities are open on Saturday mornings or even Sundays as well. To check opening hours of particular offices go to www.ctt.pt.

Mail may take up to a week to reach a European destination. There is also a three-day 'Correio Azul' (express) service.

Where's the nearest post office? **Onde fica a estação de correios mais próxima?**
A stamp for this letter/ postcard, please? **Um selo para esta carta/este postal, por favor?**
express (special delivery) **expresso**
airmail **via aérea**
registered **registado**

PUBLIC HOLIDAYS

National holidays:
1 January *Ano Novo* New Year's Day
25 April *Dia da Liberdade* Liberty Day
1 May *Festa do Trabalho* Labour Day
10 June *Dia de Portugal* National Day
15 Aug *Assunção* Assumption
5 October *Implantação da República* Republic Day
1 November *Todos-os-Santos* All Saints' Day
8 December *Imaculada Conceição* Immaculate Conception
25 December *Natal* Christmas Day
Movable dates:
Carnaval Shrove Tuesday
Sexta-feira Santa Good Friday
Corpo de Deus Corpus Christi

In addition, every town closes down and takes to the streets at least once a year in honour of its own patron saint. See the Calendar of festivals and events (page 139) for other events.

R

RELIGION

The Portuguese are predominantly Roman Catholic. The tourist information office has a list of services for English-speaking Catholics and other worshippers. Dress respectfully (avoid baring arms and legs) when visiting places of worship.

T

TELEPHONES

Portugal's country code is 351. The local area code must be dialled before all phone numbers, even for local calls (nine-digit total).

Portugal Telecom public telephones accept prepaid telephone cards and credit cards. Buy telephone cards of various denominations, starting from €3, from post offices, telephone offices and newsagents.

Local, national and international calls can also be made from hotels.

To make an international call, dial 00 for an international line (both Europe and overseas; eg UK 0044) + the country code + phone number (including the area code, without the initial '0', where there is one).

There is wide mobile phone coverage in Portugal. The major operators are Vodafone (www.vodafone.pt), MEO (www.meo.pt) and NOS (www.nos.pt).

reverse-charge call **paga pelo destinatário**
Can you get me this number in...?**Pode ligar-me para este número em...?**

TIME DIFFERENCE

Portugal is on Greenwich Mean Time. Like in the UK, from the last Sunday in March until the last Sunday in October, the clocks are moved one hour ahead for summer time, GMT + 1.

In summer the chart looks like this:

New York	London	**Lisbon**	Paris	Sydney	Auckland
7am	noon	**noon**	1pm	9pm	11pm

What time is it? **Que hora tem/é?**

TIPPING

Hotel and restaurant bills are generally all-inclusive, but an additional tip of 5–10 percent is common and even expected in restaurants. Hotel porters, per bag, generally receive at least €1. Tip taxi drivers about 10 percent.

TOILETS

Public toilets exist in some large towns, but almost every bar and restaurant has one available for public use.

Where are the toilets? **Onde é a casa de banho?**

TOURIST INFORMATION

Portuguese National Tourist Offices (ICEP or Investimentos, Comércio e Turismo de Portugal) are maintained in many countries, www.turismodeportugal.pt.

Canada: 438 University Avenue, Suite 1400, Toronto, Ontario ON M5G 2K8; tel: (416) 921 0259.
Ireland: 70 Upper Leeson Street, Dublin; tel: (353) 163 16309.
UK: Portuguese Embassy, 11 Belgrave Square, London SW1X 8PP; tel: (020) 7201 6666.
US: 866 Second Ave, 8th floor, New York, NY 10017; tel: (646) 723 0200.
In Lisbon, the main tourist information office for the city is the **Lisboa Welcome Centre**, Rua do Arsenal 15, in Praça do Comércio; tel: 210-312 700. There are also Ask Me Lisboa kiosks dotted around town. There is another office at the airport (Arrivals terminal, tel: 218 450 660). Virtually every town has a local tourist office *(turismo)*. They can provide information on sights, hotels, restaurants, transport, hospitals and police.

> Where is the tourist office? **Onde é o turismo?**

TRANSPORT

Public transport generally runs from 6am or 7am to midnight or 1am.
Local buses *(autocarros)* and **trams** *(eléctricos)*. Bus and tram stops in cities usually have a small route map and an indication of which buses stop there. You can buy your ticket on the bus, or you can buy passes or blocks of tickets from kiosks and some shops (if in doubt, ask at the tourist office or go to www.carris.pt).
Underground *(Metro)*. Lisbon has four lines, providing a fast way of getting around (www.metrolisboa.pt). Porto's Metro has more than 80 stops (www.metrodoporto.pt). On both Metro networks tickets must be validated before you get on a train.
Taxis. Most taxis are cream-coloured and have a 'taxi' sign. City taxis have meters, but are entitled to charge an extra 20 percent at weekends, public holidays and between 10pm and 6am and an extra sum (€1.60) for each item of luggage. Tip about 10 percent. If there is no meter, it is essential to establish a price before your trip starts. Most taxis use taxi stands, but

some cruise the streets looking for passengers.

Intercity buses. Intercity buses are a fairly fast, comfortable and cheap way of getting around Portugal (www.rede-expressos.pt). Buses are run by various companies, but usually operate out of the same central bus station; though in cities there can be several stations. It is worth asking for advice at the tourist office.

Trains *(comboio)*. Trains are operated by CP (Comboios de Portugal; www.cp.pt), the national rail company. Regional trains stop at most stations, intercity trains cost more and make fewer stops. Direct fast service from Porto and Lisbon to the Algarve is available on the Alfa Pendular.

Bilhete Turístico (Tourist Ticket) offers unlimited train travel on the Sintra/Azambuja, Cascais and Sado lines for 1 day or 3 days. For InterRail and Eurail passes valid in Portugal see page 167.

Lisbon is the central hub of the train network. There are four stations: Santa Apolónia for international services and to northern Portugal; Cais do Sodré for commuter trains to the western suburbs, and to Estoril and Cascais; Rossio for Sintra and the west; and Sul e Sueste for the south (including the Algarve) and the southeast (ticket prices will

Where can I get a taxi? **Onde posso encontrar um táxi?**
Can you give us a lift to...? **Pode levar-nos a...?**
What's the fare to...? **Quanto custa o percurso para...?**
Where is the nearest railway station/bus stop? **Onde é a estação ferroviária/a paragem de autocarros mais próxima?**
When's the next bus/train to...? **Quando parte o próximo autocarro/comboio para...?**
I want a ticket to... **Queria um bilhete para...**
single **ida**
return **ida e volta**
Will you tell me when to get off the bus? **Pode dizer-me quando devo descer?**

include the ferry trip across the Tagus, if necessary).

Ferries *(barcaça)*. Many boats offer services across the Tagus, up various rivers, such as the Douro and the Guadiana, to the Tróia Peninsula and to the offshore islands. Ask at local tourist offices for further details or go to www.transtejo.pt.

Domestic flights. TAP flies between Lisbon, Porto and Faro.

V

VISAS AND ENTRY REQUIREMENTS

American, British, Canadian and many other nationalities need only a valid passport – no visa – to visit Portugal. EU nationals may enter with an identity card. The length of stay authorised for most tourists is 90 days.

The Portuguese-Spanish border scarcely serves as a frontier anymore and visitors can come and go easily, though you should carry your passport.

W

WEBSITES AND INTERNET ACCESS

www.visitportugal.com official Portuguese Tourism website.

www.ana.pt official website of Portuguese airports.

www.visitalgarve.pt official Algarve region tourist website.

www.golisbon.com a complete guide to Lisbon and most attractive places in Portugal.

www.portugal-live.net comprehensive and up-to-date tourist information on Portugal.

www.theportugalnews.com news about various regions in English.

www.cp.pt Comboios de Portugal, the railway network.

Tourist offices, major commercial centres and most cafes in large cities now offer free Wi-Fi connections.

WEIGHTS AND MEASURES

Portugal uses the metric system of weights and measures.

RECOMMENDED HOTELS

Hotel prices are fairly reasonable across Portugal, though in Lisbon they have risen in recent years to match most Western European destinations, even surpassing popular cities like Barcelona at the top levels.

Room price guidelines below are rack rates for a double room with bath in high season (generally April–October), including breakfast and VAT (value-added tax – six percent of room price). All hotels except for the smallest residential inns accept major credit cards. For making reservations, Portugal's country telephone code is 351.

€€€€€	over €200
€€€€	€150–200
€€€	€100–150
€€	€60–100
€	below €60

LISBON

As Janelas Verdes €€€€€ *Rua das Janelas Verdes 47, tel: 213 968 143, booking: 213 218 200,* www.asjanelasverdes.com. Charming, elegant hotel in the chic Lapa district, near the River Tagus and Museu de Arte Antiga. This small hotel occupies the 18th-century townhouse of one of Portugal's most famous writers, Eço de Queirós, plus the neighbouring house. Has a quiet courtyard and top-floor library, and some rooms have superb views of the river. Wheelchair access. 29 rooms.

Bairro Alto Hotel €€€€€ *Praça Luis de Camoé 2, tel: 213 408 288,* www.bairroaltohotel.com. Ultra chic hotel in the old heart of Lisbon. Rooms have plasma TV and are soundproofed. Upmarket styling and prices. 55 rooms.

Hotel Avenida Palace €€€€ *Rua 1 de Dezembro 123, tel: 213 218 100,* www.hotelavenidapalace.pt. Right on Rossio, the major plaza in the

Baixa district, the remodelled Avenida Palace is one of Lisbon's finest luxury hotels. Magnificent Old World feel. Disabled access. Regular jazz and classical music concerts. 82 rooms.

Hotel Britania €€€€ *Rua Rodrigues Sampaio 17, tel: 213 155 016,* www. heritage.pt. A 1940s townhouse with spacious, elegantly appointed bedrooms. Original art deco interior has been lovingly restored. Disabled access. 32 rooms.

Hotel do Chiado €€€€ *Rua Nova do Almada 114, tel: 213 256 100,* www. hoteldochiado.com. Situated in the heart of the upmarket Chiado district and previously known as the Lisboa Regency Chiado, this is sleekly stylish, with superb views over Alfama from the roof terrace. Chic lobby and rooms. Disabled access. 40 rooms.

Olissippo Lapa Palace €€€€€ *Rua Pau da Bandeira 4, tel: 213 949 494,* www.olissippohotels.com. Fine conversion of a palatial old mansion overlooking the River Tagus in Lapa. Landscaped gardens and outdoor pool. Plush rooms. Disabled access. 109 rooms.

Hotel Metropole €€€ *Praça D. Pedro IV 30 (Rossio), tel: 213 219 030.* One of Lisbon's best deals is this classic, art deco 1920s hotel in a square surrounded by historic buildings in the heart of the Baixa. Large rooms, 16 with castle, Baixa and Alfama views. Disabled access. 36 rooms.

VIP Executive Suites Éden €€€ *Praça dos Restauradores 24, tel: 213 216 600,* www.viphotels.com. Located in a famous art deco building on Praça dos Restauradores, this modern apartment-hotel is a great deal, especially for families. There are kitchen-equipped studios and full apartments, with daily or weekly maid service. Panoramic rooftop pool and breakfast service. Wheelchair access. 134 rooms.

York House €€€€–€€€€€ *Rua das Janelas Verdes 32, tel: 213 962 435,* www.yorkhouselisboa.com. Historic hotel set within a converted 17th-century convent near the Museum of Ancient Art. Elegant, sleek rooms. Good restaurant. Disabled access. 32 rooms.

ESTORIL COAST

Casa da Pergola €€€€ *Avenida Valbom 13, 2750 Cascais, tel: 214 840 040*, www.pergolahouse.pt. Glorious, family-run old manor house B&B, set in pretty gardens, with a grand marble staircase and rooms full of wood-carved and rococo antiques. Several have balconies overlooking the garden. 10 rooms.

Hotel Albatroz €€€–€€€€€ *Rua Frederico Arouca 100, 2750 Cascais, tel: 214 847 380*, www.albatrozhotels.com. Cascais's most elegant hotel is this mansion perched above the Praia da Rainha beach. Rooms are very luxurious. Outdoor pool and lovely gardens. Pleasant restaurant with good seafood. Disabled access. 51 rooms.

NEAR LISBON

Pousada de Setúbal, São Filipe €€€€ *Forte de São Filipe, 2900 Setúbal, tel: 265 550 070*, www.pousadas.pt. Luxury *pousada* inside the walls of a fortress from 1590, overlooking the port of Setúbal. Great views. Near the Serra de Arrábida National Park. 16 rooms.

Tivoli Palacio de Seteais €€€€ *Rua Barbosa do Bocage, 8, 2710 Sintra, tel: 219 233 200*, www.minorhotels.com. Set on the hills of Sintra, this luxurious 18th century palace hotel offers spectacular views over the historic town. Its 30 elegant rooms and ballrooms are decorated with tapestries and frescos.

RIBATEJO & ESTEMADURA

Hotel dos Templários €€€ *Largo Cândido dos Reis 1, 2304-909 Tomar, tel: 249 310 100*, www.hoteldostemplarios.pt. A large hotel on the banks of the river. Spacious rooms – all with terraces, some with views of the Convento de Cristo. Indoor swimming pool and tennis court, health club. Disabled access. 177 rooms.

Pousada de Óbidos, Castelo de Óbidos €€€€ *Paço Real, 2510-999 Óbidos, tel: 210 407 630*, www.pousadas.pt. As is common across Portugal, this charming *pousada* is fashioned from an historic monument, the medieval castle inside the walled town. Stunning views and celebrated restaurant. A couple of two-storey suites are in castle towers. Reserve well in advance. 9 rooms.

Granja do Vallado €€ *Rua Carlos O'Neil 20, 2450-344 Nazaré, tel: 912 544 151*, www.granjadovallado.com. Family-run, large 600-year-old manor house, 5km (3 miles) from Nazaré. Swimming pool, tennis court, bicycles to hire and gardens. 8 rooms.

THE BEIRAS

Bussaco Palace Hotel €€€€ *Mata do Bussaco, 3050 Luso, tel: 231 937 970*, www.almeidahotels.pt. Palatial hotel, built as a hunting retreat for the last kings of Portugal. In the legendary Buçaco forest. Good restaurant (see page 151). 64 rooms.

Quinta das Lágrimas €€€€ *Rua António Augusto Gonçalves, 3041 Coimbra, tel: 239 802 380*, www.quintadaslagrimas.pt. The 'House of Tears' is an 18th-century palace on 4 hectares (10 acres) of gardens and woods across the river from old Coimbra. Prince Pedro and Inêz de Castro are said to have conducted their love affair here in the 14th century. Handsomely decorated rooms, excellent restaurant (see page 151). 54 rooms.

Yurt Holiday Portugal €€ *Lugar Varzeas, Pracerias, Celavisa, 3300-207 Arganil, tel: 235 208 562*, www.yurtholidayportugal.com. Beautifully appointed, antique-decorated yurts on a remote organic smallholding in the mountains of central Portugal, surrounded by olives, vines and fruit trees.

PORTO AND THE DOURO VALLEY

Castelo Santa Catarina €€€ *Rua Santa Catarina 1347, 4000-457 Porto, tel: 225 095 599*, www.castelosantacatarina.com.pt. Extravagant and amazing, this castle-like, tile-covered place has bags of charm, though rooms are variable and some are better and more characterful than others. 25 rooms.

Hotel Infante Sagres €€€€€ *Praça D. Filipa de Lencastre 62, 4050-259 Porto, tel: 223 398 500,* www.hotelinfantesagres.pt. Luxury hotel in the centre of Porto. Though it appears to be from an earlier age, it was built in 1951. Good service, handsome public rooms, swish superior rooms, and nice restaurant. Disabled access. 70 rooms.

Pestana Vintage Porto Hotel €€€€ *Praça da Ribeira, 1, 4050-513 Porto, tel: 223 402 300,* www.pestana.com. A small boutique hotel ideally located in Ribeira, right on the waterfront. Rooms are sleekly modern and comfortable, but vary in shape and size. Many have superb views of the Dom Luís bridge and river. Disabled access. 48 rooms.

Pousada Solar da Rede €€€–€€€€ *Santa Cristina, 5040 Mesão Frio, tel: 254 890 130.* With stunning views over the River Douro, this gracious 18th-century manor house has orchards and a 27-hectare (67-acre) vineyard. Regal furnishings and public rooms. Swimming pool, tennis court. 31 rooms.

Vintage House €€€ *Lugar da Ponte, 5085 Pinhão, tel: 254 730 230,* www.csvintagehouse.com. Vintage House is a lovely country house-style hotel. It has luxurious traditional styling, a superb restaurant and library bar. Tennis court, swimming pool. Disabled access. 43 rooms.

THE MINHO

Albergaria Bracara Augusta €€€€ *Avenida Central 134, 4710-229 Braga, tel: 253 206 260,* www.bracaraaugusta.com. This central converted townhouse offers graceful, light rooms with polished wood floors and pretty balconies. Staff are helpful and friendly. Good restaurant. 19 rooms.

Pousada de Guimarães, Santa Marinha €€€–€€€€ *Laro Domingos Leite Castro, 4810-011 Guimarães, tel: 253 511 249,* www.pousadas.pt. Stunningly converted 12th-century monastery in the Penha hills 3km (2 miles) from Guimarães. Beautiful antiques and art throughout, spectacular cloister and gardens, great views of Guimarães. 51 rooms.

Pousada de Viana do Castelo, Monte de Santa Luzia €€€ *Santa Luzia, 4901-909 Viana do Castelo, tel: 258 800 370*, www.pousadas.pt. Peaceful 1930s hotel perched on a hill overlooking the resort town of Viana, River Lima and the Atlantic. Tennis court, secluded swimming pool, gardens. 50 rooms.

Pousada do Gerês-Amares, Santa Maria do Bouro €€€–€€€€ *Largo do Terreiro Santa Maria do Bouro, 4720-633 Amares, tel: 253 371 971/2/3*, www.pousadas.pt. Daring modern adaptation of a former Cistercian monastery between Braga and the Gerês mountain range. Sleek furnishings, exposed medieval stone walls. Beautiful bar and dining room. Disabled access. 32 rooms.

Quinta do Paço de Calheiros €€€ *Calvário, Calheiros, 4990-575 Ponte de Lima, tel: 258 947 164*, www.pacodecalheiros.com. Sumptuous rural inn in terraced fields above the river, 7km (4 miles) from Ponte de Lima. Rooms and the seven lush apartments are beautifully furnished. Horse-riding, tennis and swimming pool. 16 rooms.

Residencial Dora € *Largo Senhora-a-Branha, 92-94, 700-962 Braga, tel: 253 200 180*, www.hotelresidencialdora.com. This modest hotel offers good value for money. Simple rooms are small but clean. In high season prices include breakfast with a choice of pastries. Friendly service.

TRÁS-OS-MONTES

Forte de São Francisco €€€ *Alto da Pedisqueira, 5400-435 Chaves, tel: 276 333 700*, www.fortesaofrancisco.com. A marvellously converted 16th-century convent within the Fortress of São Francisco, with large rooms, handsome furnishings and details. There is an excellent restaurant and a tavern for informal meals. Tennis court, sauna. Disabled access. 58 rooms.

Pousada de Bragança, São Bartolomeu €€€ *5300-271 Bragança, tel: 273 331 493*, www.pousadas.pt. Comfortable modern pousada on a hill overlooking the Bragança citadel. Large rooms with pleasant terraces. Disabled access. 28 rooms.

ALENTEJO

Hotel Convento de São Paulo €€€€ *Aldeia da Serra, 7170-120 Redondo, tel: 266 989 160,* www.hotelconventosaopaulo.com. Convent dating from 1128 between Estremoz and Évora on the slopes of the D'Ossa mountains, among 600 hectares (1,483 acres) of woodlands and gardens. Long corridors are lined with 50,000 *azulejo* tiles. Excellent restaurant with vaulted ceilings and 18th-century frescoes. 32 rooms.

Pousada de Estremoz, Rainha Santa Isabel €€€€ *Largo de D. Diniz, 7100-509 Estremoz, tel: 268 332 075,* www.pousadas.pt. An inn inside Estremoz castle (which King Dinis built for his Queen, Santa Isabel) with museum-quality furnishings throughout, beautiful gardens and a swimming pool enclosed by ramparts. 29 rooms.

Pousada de Vila Viçosa, Dom João IV €€€–€€€€ *Terreiro do Paço, 7160-251 Vila Viçosa, tel: 268 980 742,* www.pousadas.pt. Located right next door to the royal palace of the Dukes of Bragança in what was formerly a 16th-century convent. Traditional style, with large rooms and central courtyard. Swimming pool. Disabled access. 39 rooms.

Pousada do Crato, Flor da Rosa €€€€ *7430-999 Crato, tel: 245 997 210/1,* www.pousadas.pt. Architectural showpiece, a starkly modern conversion of a ruined 14th-century castle and convent. Sleek furnishings and brilliant use of space. Large rooms, three in the tower, and beautiful pool. Free internet access in public areas. Disabled access. 25 rooms.

Pousada Évora, Convento dos Lóios €€€€ *Largo Conde de Vila Flor, 7000-804 Évora, tel: 266 730 070,* www.pousadas.pt. Luxurious 15th-century convent next to the Roman Temple. Antique furnishings. Chic restaurant, outdoor pool. Spa, reading room and free internet. 33 rooms.

THE ALGARVE

Hotel Marina Rio €€€ *Avenida dos Descobrimentos, 8600-645 Lagos, tel: 282 780 830,* www.marinario.com. With great marina views, this smart little place has rooms (all twins) with balconies. There's a small pool on the rooftop. 36 rooms.

Estalagem Abrigo da Montanha €€–€€€ *Corte Pereiro, 8550-257 Monchique, tel: 282 912 131,* www.abrigodamontanha.com. High up in the Serra de Monchique, lies this wood-and-granite mountain lodge retreat. Pretty rooftop pool and café-restaurant just across the road. Perfect for hikers. 14 rooms.

Hotel Quinta do Lago €€€€ *Quinta do Lago, 8135-024 Almancil, tel: 289 390 700,* www.quintadolago.com. A standard bearer for luxury and leisure situated in 810 hectares (2,000 acres) of gardens and woods. Features three golf courses to rotate between set alongside the Ria Formosa Nature Preserve. Water sports, health club, pools and lovely beach. Disabled access. 141 rooms.

Tivoli Lagos €€€€ *Rua António Crisógono dos Santos, 8600-678 Lagos, tel: 282 790 079,* www.minorhotels.com. Large hotel with character in the old part of Lagos. Gardens, attractive poolside areas, indoor swimming pool, three restaurants, health club, tennis courts. Free shuttle service takes guests to the Duna Beach Club. 324 rooms.

Pestana Alvor Praia €€€€ *Praia de Três Irmãos, 8501-904 Alvor, tel: 282 400 900,* www.pestana.com. Large and luxurious, this hotel is set among thick trees and gardens on cliffs, overlooking fine beaches. Features Olympic-size saltwater pool with ocean views. Three restaurants with terraces and different cuisines. Tennis courts, full spa. Disabled access. 195 rooms.

Pousada de Tavira, Convento da Graça €€€€ *Rua D. Paio Peres Correia, 8800-407 Tavira, tel: 281 407 680,* www.pousadas.pt. Another historic convent in the *pousadas* group. Some 13th-century archaeological treasures of Islamic origin were discovered during the refurbishing of the hotel. There's alfresco dining on an arcaded terrace, and a swimming pool. Disabled access. 36 rooms.

Residencial Praia do Vau €€ Apartado 158, 8501 Portimão, tel: 282 401 312. Small, rustic inn in an attractive, characteristic Algarve house just

200 metres/yds from the Praia do Vau beach (west of Praia da Rocha); includes four apartments. 21 rooms.

Pine Cliffs Hotel €€€€ *Praia da Falésia, 8200-909 Albufeira, tel: 289 500 100,* www.pinecliffshotel.com. Surrounded by pines at the top of dramatic cliffs, the Sheraton Algarve Hotel features handsome Moorish styling, excellent restaurants and extensive sporting facilities, including the Pine Cliffs nine-hole golf course and golf academy. Great facilities for children. Six pools. Disabled access. 215 rooms.

Vila Channa €€€ *Caminho des Sesmarias, São Rafael, 8200 Albufeira, tel: 289 592 354.* A pleasant, spotless, villa-style small hotel, which is just a short walk from a couple of the prettiest beaches near Albufeira, Castelo and São Rafael. Well appointed pool. 18 rooms.

Vila Joya €€€€ *Estrada da Galé, 8200-416 Albufeira, tel: 289 591 795,* www.vilajoya.com. Stylish Moorish-influenced villa just minutes from calm Galé beach. Beautiful rooms. Most rooms have glorious sea views. Reserve months in advance. 20 rooms.

INDEX

INSIGHT ⊙ GUIDES POCKET GUIDE

PORTUGAL

First Edition 2018

Editor: Sian Marsh
Author: Neil Schlecht, Abigail Blasi
Head of Production: Rebeka Davies
Picture Editor: Tom Smyth
Cartography Update: Carte
Update Production: Apa Digital
Photography Credits: Bigstock 15, 94;
Corbis 53; Getty Images 24; iStock 5MC, 33,
38, 41, 51, 67, 73, 77, 78, 82, 86, 105, 121,
122; Lydia Evans/Apa Publications 4MC,
4ML, 4TL, 5T, 5TC, 5M, 6L, 6R, 7, 7R, 11, 13,
16, 18, 21, 23, 28, 30, 32, 35, 36, 42, 45, 46,
48, 55, 56, 59, 60, 63, 65, 68, 69, 71, 74, 81,
84, 89, 91, 92, 96, 98, 101, 102, 106, 108, 111,
112, 115, 117, 119, 124, 126, 128, 131, 132,
134, 137, 140, 142, 144, 146; Shutterstock 1,
4TC, 5MC, 5M, 40
Cover Picture: iStock

Distribution
UK, Ireland and Europe: Apa Publications
(UK) Ltd; sales@insightguides.com
United States and Canada: Ingram
Publisher Services; ips@ingramcontent.com
Australia and New Zealand: Woodslane;
info@woodslane.com.au
Southeast Asia: Apa Publications (SN) Pte;
singaporeoffice@insightguides.com
Worldwide: Apa Publications (UK) Ltd;
sales@insightguides.com

**Special Sales, Content Licensing
and CoPublishing**
Insight Guides can be purchased in bulk
quantities at discounted prices. We can
create special editions, personalised jackets
and corporate imprints tailored to your
needs. sales@insightguides.com;
www.insightguides.biz

Contact us
Every effort has been made to provide
accurate information in this publication,
but changes are inevitable. The publisher
cannot be responsible for any resulting loss,
inconvenience or injury. We would appreciate
it if readers would call our attention to any
errors or outdated information. We also
welcome your suggestions; please contact
us at: hello@insightguides.com
www.insightguides.com

INSIGHT ⦿ GUIDES

OFF THE SHELF

Since 1970, INSIGHT GUIDES has provided a unique perspective on the world's best travel destinations by using specially commissioned photography and illuminating text written by local authors.

Whether you're planning a city break, a walking tour or the journey of a lifetime, our superb range of guidebooks and phrasebooks will inspire you to discover more about your chosen destination.

INSIGHT GUIDES

offer a unique combination of stunning photos, absorbing narrative and detailed maps, providing all the inspiration and information you need.

PHRASEBOOKS & DICTIONARIES

help users to feel at home, when away. Pocket-sized with a free app to download, they go where you do.

CITY GUIDES

pack hundreds of great photos into a smaller format with detailed practical information, so you can navigate the world's top cities with confidence.

EXPLORE GUIDES

feature easy-to-follow walks and itineraries in the world's most exciting destinations, with our choice of the best places to eat and drink along the way.

POCKET GUIDES

combine concise information on where to go and what to do in a handy compact format, ideal on the ground. Includes a full-colour, fold-out map.

EXPERIENCE GUIDES

feature offbeat perspectives and secret gems for experienced travellers, with a collection of over 100 ideas for a memorable stay in a city.

www.insightguides.com